RIGOROUS READING

5 Access Points for Comprehending Complex Texts

TEXAS EDITION

DOUGLAS FISHER
NANCY FREY

FOREWORD BY GRETCHEN BERNABEI

FOR INFORMATION:

Corwin

A SAGE Company

2455 Teller Road

Thousand Oaks, California 91320

(800) 233-9936

www.corwin.com

SAGE Publications Ltd.

1 Oliver's Yard

55 City Road

London EC1Y 1SP

United Kingdom

SAGE Publications India Pvt. Ltd.

B 1/I 1 Mohan Cooperative Industrial Area

Mathura Road, New Delhi 110 044

India

SAGE Publications Asia-Pacific Pte. Ltd.

3 Church Street

#10-04 Samsung Hub

Singapore 049483

Publisher and Senior Program Director: Lisa Luedeke

Editorial Development Manager: Julie Nemer

Editorial Assistant: Sharon Wu

Production Editor: David C. Felts

Copy Editor: Kim Husband

Typesetter: C&M Digitals (P) Ltd.

Proofreader: Jeff Bryant

Indexer: Sheila Bodell

Cover Designer: Janet Kiesel

Marketing Managers: Rebecca Eaton, Brian Grimm

Printed in the United States of America

ISBN 978-1-5443-3635-0

This book is printed on acid-free paper.

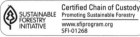

SUSTAINABLE FORESTRY INITIATIVE

Certified Chain of Custody
Promoting Sustainable Forestry
www.sfiprogram.org
SFI-01268

SFI label applies to text stock

18 19 20 21 22 10 9 8 7 6 5 4 3 2 1

What Your Colleagues Are Saying

"This is a bold book. . . . It is genius, and its unique contribution, is in bringing the balance and the centeredness to new education standards."

—P. DAVID PEARSON
University of California, Berkeley

"With *Rigorous Reading*, Doug Fisher and Nancy Frey have provided literacy educators who are committed to successfully raising the bar with solutions that make sense. The book is masterfully developed with an extensive reach across many grade levels in terms of defining what it means to provide intentional instruction and teaching text complexity. The five access points are discussed pragmatically with evidence of a solid research base deftly woven throughout the book. This is the most practical book I have come across in terms of providing teachers with the knowledge base and assistance many are seeking to improve their instruction with regard to complex texts."

—STEVEN L. LAYNE, EdD
Professor of Literacy Education, Judson University
and Author of *Igniting a Passion for Reading*

"In *Rigorous Reading: 5 Access Points for Comprehending Complex Texts,* Fisher and Frey help teachers understand how to bring vigor to rigor. They teach us how to help students understand more from their complex texts—greater understanding that will help to bring life and energy to each student's reading. Rooted in solid research, this is book is a must-read for those grappling with how to translate the recommendations and mandates around text complexity into instructional practices."

—JENNIFER SERRAVALLO
Author of *Teaching Reading in Small Groups* and
Conferring with Readers

"[W]e need resources that show us how to support students in developing their full literacy potential. In this very practical and insightful book, Fisher and Frey examine how conceptions of text complexity are causing us to shift some of our ideas about reading instruction. *Rigorous Reading* is an important resource that will help teachers align reading instruction in powerful ways."

—LINDA B. GAMBRELL
Professor, Clemson University

RIGOROUS READING

TEXAS EDITION

Contents

CHAPTER 3. Access Point Two: Close and Scaffolded Reading Instruction

CHAPTER 6. Access Point Five: Assessing Students' Understanding

Visit the companion website at
resources.corwin.com/rigorousreadingtx
for access to video clips and other resources.

■ ■ ■

Note From the Publisher: *The authors have provided video and web content throughout the book that is available to you through QR (quick response) codes. To read a QR code, you must have a smartphone or tablet with a camera. We recommend that you download a QR code reader app that is made specifically for your phone or tablet brand.*

List of Videos

Access the following videos at **resources.corwin.com/rigorousreadingtx**.

Chapter 1

Video 1.1 Doug discusses text complexity.
Video 1.2 Nancy reviews a text for the factors of complexity.
Video 1.3 Doug discusses close reading.
Video 1.4 Teacher uses questioning techniques to aid student comprehension.
Video 1.5 Teacher modeling comprehension strategies.
Video 1.6 Doug talks about the gradual release of responsibility.

Chapter 2

Video 2.1 A teacher models for her students.
Video 2.2 An elementary teacher models word solving.
Video 2.3 A high school teacher models word solving.
Video 2.4 Making Learning Visible through Learning Intentions.

Chapter 3

Video 3.1 Close reading with sixth-grade English language learners.
Video 3.2 Students rereading and discussing a complex text in high school English.
Video 3.3 Close reading of historical information.
Video 3.4 Close reading and text-dependent questions in upper elementary school.
Video 3.5 Close reading in the primary grades.
Video 3.6 Teacher working with groups of students to facilitate their understanding.
Video 3.7 Teacher using prompts and cues to guide learning.

Foreword

Dear Texas Teacher,

Let me take you back in time. Back before STAAR, back before TAKS or TAAS, before TEAMS. Back to the 80s, to our very first large-scale, state-sponsored test. The TABS test. Texas Assessment of Basic Skills. It was completely multiple choice, crudely manufactured, and I was young, acclimating to my new role as a ninth grade teacher in Elgin, Texas. At the encouragement of our administrators, we scrambled to help students who failed. In the next year, my sister Sue was hired at my school to be a "TABS teacher." Remediation for a test was a new concept, and she grappled with her options for helping kids at our high school. I remember looking with her at the questions on the test, neatly categorized into "identifying main idea," "determining important details," "inferencing," "summarizing." It felt alien, only mildly connected to the act of reading, definitely unrelated to any of our experiences as readers. But hey—we were open to learning.

We couldn't have known we were at the dawn of an era of splintered reading and writing instruction, an era papered with billions of dollars' worth of malnourishing materials that would not serve Texas students across the state. Practice tests would reign, and novels would be replaced with skills of the week. From Texarkana to Laredo, students would bubble in answers about main idea. From McAllen to Amarillo, students would endure endless drills on inferencing. Across this land, we people at schools tried to convert our impossibly subjective text responses into impossibly worded answer choices to preposterously written objective questions.

Yep, reform had arrived. And within a few decades of wildly growing testing programs (yes! whole programs!), we would see unfettered legislation, mandating increasingly dire consequences for poor performances. The result? Mounting test-prep frenzy. The need for reform had become the need for rescue.

Now let's think about what we know about reading, by thinking about what we see in our students' reading lives. Here are some truisms I've come to believe from observing my classroom, from grades 6–12. Some of them are painful.

- Many students in Texas consider themselves uninterested in reading.
- Good readers have obvious mental conversations with difficult texts.
- Predictable mental conversations are never obvious to readers who don't know how to have them.
- In teaching, showing is more effective than telling.
- Students need a range of tools to use with texts.
- Teachers need a range of tools to use with students.
- Most teachers don't feel competent teaching reading or writing strategically.
- We need to grow our readers.

At first glance, students might look briefly at a tough text, decide it's too hard, and mentally make a U-turn.

At first glance, teachers might decide that their students just aren't getting it and do the same U-turn.

Reading dense, complex texts is hard. And teaching students to do it is even harder. How often teachers hear "I hate reading." Sometimes students seem locked-up tight in their identity as a non-reader, and the teacher's challenge is to find chinks in that armor, openings.

I confess that I was one of those readers. In sharp contrast to my sister Sue, who devoured Jane Austen at 9, the Brontës at 10, Melville at 11, I stayed true to Archie, Betty, and Veronica. Sure, I glanced into her books occasionally, only to confirm that—ew. I don't like reading.

Years later in college, I was thrown against my will into the only class offered in my time slot, a class in John Milton. Great. A whole class to study the writing of John Nauseating Milton. During the first real class period, our professor had us turn to a poem, short by Miltonian standards, but incomprehensible nonetheless. He asked us to get into groups, read it, and make sense of it. My group and I sat there, staring at the tangled twist of language, unable to form a single mental image, unable to unjumble the allusions, a hopeless mass of queasy bewilderment (us, not the poem). We were flummoxed, lost. Humiliated, I approached my professor, who sat unconcerned but possibly watching us behind his newspaper.

"Dr. Milton?" (That's how I remember his name, though it wasn't.) "We don't know how to do this."

He looked at me with a twinkle. "Try finding the subjects and the verbs," he murmured and turned back to his paper. I was startled. Oh. The subjects and the verbs. I could do that.

If I had witnessed the Northern Lights, I may not have experienced the epiphany that came with the search for subjects and verbs. The language untangled and a story emerged:

> In blah blah blah, with blah blah blah, **the young maidens**
> with blah blah blah, from the blah blah to blah blah, like blah
> blah on blah blah, **ran** as blah blah **and frolicked** blah blah.

I didn't understand all of it, but now I had a toehold in the impenetrable language.

And through the days of that class, I did learn to take bigger bites, to recognize spicy devices and sweet nuances, and it doesn't matter so much that I'm now the biggest Milton fan I know; what matters to me, and the lesson I have carried with me, is what happened to me as a reader the moment that professor gave me one concrete way in. One way into the text.

I didn't know what to call it until I read this book. Now I know he gave me an *access point*.

This book offers teachers five wide access points to build kids' abilities, equipping us with gentle and natural ways to find chinks in the armor, cracks in the wall, toeholds into which students can build their own resilient competencies as readers. None of the access points will be unfamiliar to you, but you will find yourself thinking about these in different ways, via concrete help, concrete tools, and concrete illustrations.

The five are:

1. Modeling our thought processes while reading, most notably with thinkalouds. It's the same process that writers afford readers, the invitation into the mental workings of someone else. It's personal and juicy. And most importantly, the way the Douglas Fisher and Nancy Frey model this, the learner gains some templates, sentence stems, or text structures for immediate use, like this: "I read this part, and I'm confused about this…but I notice this…which makes me think this…."

2. Instruction in close reading and scaffolded reading. The authors clarify the difference, generously sharing tips that resonate as forehead-slapping common sense, like limiting the front-loading before students read a piece. They pay special attention in this section to annotating.

3. Leading students to have collaborative conversations with peers. This is what Dr. Milton had us do to help us unpack that poem back in college. It can help your students, too. One of my new favorite methods here is "clink, clunk, and get the gist."

4. Weaving together daily servings of (easier) SSR and (tougher) independent close reading. The authors separate for us the roles of these two: SSR as pure pleasure reading, without logging or tedious responses to slow down the fluency-building, enjoyment-storing habits; close reading instruction, using selections that students might not choose on their own.

5. Assessing understanding mostly through performance of some kind. This section clearly validates what seems creative and fun for students, whether it is an essay, a debate, or other performance, and where reader response gets to act up.

Doug Fisher and Nancy Frey have laid out for us an organic range of choices for teachers to use, designing learning experiences and routines for all kids. They add their voices to ours as colleagues, showing us that the most powerful tools we have in our classrooms are our own eyes as we watch our students, and our own sense of what to do next. They teach their students how to regulate their own processes, and they lead us similarly to regulate our own teaching processes.

I challenge you to read this book twice—once looking for things you know how to do already as a reader and as a teacher. The second time, read it looking for new ways in, as a teacher. And as you read, try to remember what it was like before you were competent at reading dense text. You might discover your own toeholds, just as I did.

And as for test scores, here are a couple of a certainties: we will probably have tests as long as we have Texas. But if our students are deeply growing as readers and writers, test scores will occupy only a side glance of our time with our students. From San Antonio to Livingston, from Orange to Sweetwater, we will spend the rest of our class time as we should, with texts and conversations that matter.

Gretchen Bernabei
Author of *Fun-Size Academic Writing for Serious Learning, Grammar Keepers, Text Structures From Nursery Rhymes,* and *Text Structures From the Masters*

Introduction: Your Access Point

Perhaps it was the title that caught your eye: *Rigorous Reading, Texas Edition: 5 Access Points for Comprehending Complex Texts*. There are several phrases embedded in the title, any one of which could have resonated with you.

We chose *Rigorous Reading* because the language of the Texas standards has made it clear that our students are expected to engage regularly with complex texts. A first step toward doing so is in understanding exactly what makes a given text complex. Quantitative and qualitative measures of literary and informational texts are prompting our field to examine more closely the factors that contribute to text complexity. We stand on the shoulders of giants like William S. Gray, Jeanne Chall, Edward Fry, Elfrieda Hiebert, and so many others who have made it their lives' work to help us understand how a text works. In the past, we have been content to leave these determinations up to others. Now, we are ready to assume more responsibility for understanding what the numbers on the book cover mean. We are growing in our ability to perceive the nuances that make some texts more complex than others, especially in divining those qualities that only a knowledgeable human reader can perceive.

But knowing the breadth and depth of a text is not sufficient, and perhaps you picked up this book because the word *Comprehend* captured your attention. That's not surprising—did you know that reading comprehension studies are the oldest in the field of educational research? The earliest use of the term *comprehension* as it relates to reading was by J. Russell Webb in his *Normal Series of School Readers to Teach Correct Reading*, published in 1856. (By the way, the full title also promised to *Improve and Expand the Mind and Purify and Elevate the Character*.) Comprehension is fundamental in reading, and in this book. Without deep understanding, complex texts are inanimate objects. It is only in the reader's mind that a book comes to life. It is truly wondrous that the physical limitations of time and space vanish when a reader engages in silent dialogue with a writer. As teachers of reading, we want to share what Beatrix Potter imagined from her garden in the English countryside. As teachers of literacy in the disciplines, we want to make it possible for Aristotle's formal logic to come to life in the mind of a 21st century adolescent. Maybe J. Russell Webb was right after all.

Chances are good, though, that the phrase *Helping Students* was the clincher. The five access points we discuss in this book form its center. It would be woefully inadequate to simply fill a room with complex texts and believe that was enough. If it were, we could simply park our students for a decade or so in the great libraries in our schools and communities. But communing with Potter and Aristotle, not to mention Junot Diaz, Chinua Achebe, Basho, and Zu Chongzhi, is not possible without granting students access to these ideas. The five access points build a bridge between the reader and the text and are accomplished through intentional instruction:

1. Establishing reasons for reading a complex text, and modeling how an expert reader (you) makes meaning
2. Providing scaffolded and close reading instruction to guide students through complex texts
3. Creating opportunities for collaborative conversations between students to refine their understanding
4. Moving them forward through independent reading of increasingly complex texts
5. Using formative assessment opportunities so you and the reader know what is known, and what is not yet known

We wrote this book with access in mind, and our intention is to provide you with a road map for ensuring that all the students you work with, both now and in the future, can come to know what we collectively have known: The world of texts, whether print or digital, represents a history of our past and the promise of our future. Given that imperative, is there anything more important we can do than to open up access for children and adolescents? In a word—WELCOME.

Ramping Up for Complex Texts

Helping students read more and better has always been the goal of literacy educators. In our profession, we've tried all kinds of approaches to ensure that students can read and understand the wide range of texts they will be confronted with as they grow and develop. There have been times in our history when students were assigned to read hard texts independently. The thinking at the time was that exposure to great works alone would result in learned citizens. That didn't work because students found summaries that they could use to answer comprehension questions and write essays, although it certainly spawned a whole new publishing category: commercial study guides. Doug remembers being assigned to read *Antigone* and searching everywhere for CliffsNotes so that he could complete the required worksheets and write his essay in response to this prompt:

Identify the tragic hero of one of the plays. Analyze the scenes in which the character displays pride and identify the effects that this pride has on the character's life. How could his/her life have been different if he/she had behaved in a less prideful manner?

Just giving students complex text doesn't mean they will read and understand it.

Thankfully, the answers to this question were clearly articulated in the yellow- and black-striped book. It wasn't that Doug didn't want to read *Antigone*, but rather that although he was assigned to read it, he wasn't taught how to understand an ancient Greek play such that he could answer this prompt. Unfortunately, his teacher did not know that he hadn't read the play because he earned an A on the essay. Lesson learned: Just giving students complex text doesn't mean they will read and understand it.

At other times, we've scaffolded so much that we removed the need for students to read altogether. That didn't work because students were not applying what they had learned to new texts. Nancy remembers a teacher telling her class so much about each assigned chapter of *The Secret Garden* that Nancy didn't feel the need to read the book at all, and spent her time reading Nancy Drew mysteries instead. She was able to complete all of the tasks (and please her teacher) because the teacher did the majority of the work. The fact that Nancy participated eagerly in classroom discussions wasn't an indication that she was a good reader but rather that she was a good listener. Her teacher's recounting of the previous night's chapter was sufficient for Nancy to engage in rich and collaborative discussions.

Neither of these approaches met the intended goal of getting students to read complex texts. Instead, they relied on either too little, or too much, teaching. To ensure that students actually do learn to read complex texts, teachers have to scaffold instruction and know when to transfer the cognitive and metacognitive responsibility to students. They need to rethink the texts they use, expanding the range to include more complex texts accompanied by scaffolds and support. And they need to carefully consider the intentional instruction students need to receive if they are going to apply what they have learned to the wide world of texts available to them.

In this chapter, we focus on two major concepts in literacy instruction: text complexity and close reading. Given the new *Texas Standard Knowledge & Skills for English Language Arts and Reading* (Adapted 2017), you are likely concerned with making it possible for students to read increasingly complex texts and to gain exposure to thoughtful reading instruction that provides access to these texts. Therefore, the first section will address text complexity. The second section will examine the need for students to read these texts closely, critically, and deeply. Starting in Kindergarten, text complexity and close and critical reading are important. As the standards note, "As skills and knowledge are obtained in each of the seven strands, students will continue to apply earlier standards with greater depth to increasingly complex texts in multiple genres as they become self-directed, critical learners who work collaboratively while continuously using metacognitive skills." The final portion of the chapter is an introduction to a gradual release of responsibility instructional framework that provides the access points students require to access complex texts.

▶ Reading Complex Texts

The conversation about text complexity has increased in importance since 2010. New expectations for text difficulty have been created, as we will discuss in what follows. Having said that, it is important to note that the Texas standards do not provide explicit expectations for the rigor of texts. But it's equally important to note that students will be assessed with appropriately complex texts, and their success in college and in careers will be dependent on reading proficiency. Consider, for example the evidence presented by Wei, Cromwell, and McClarty (2016) in their study of text complexity levels of occupational reading materials. They divided occupations into zones based on the level of education provided. For example, Zone 1 required little higher education and included jobs such as food preparation workers, taxi drivers, and food servers. Zone 5, the highest, included jobs for which a master's degree was generally required and included positions such as nutritionist, lawyer, and pharmacist. They collected a variety of texts, such as training guides, reference aids, and handbooks. The average reading level for Zone 1 jobs was grade 11.2 (or about 1300 Lexile), with a high of 13.9. Zone 5 jobs averaged at 13.8 (or about 1450 Lexile), with a high of 14. In fact, the authors conclude that the average text complexity demands for careers in each job zone are higher than most state standards expect of 9th and 10th graders. In their words, "even jobs that require no formal schooling beyond high school still involve comprehension of texts at the level that should be present at the end of high school," which they identify as a Lexile reading level of between 1150 and 1350.

To ensure that students actually do learn to read complex texts, teachers have to scaffold instruction and know when to transfer the cognitive and metacognitive responsibility to students.

The standards also note that requires students to read "increasingly complex texts" serves as a reminder that the ability to make meaning is the ultimate goal and that carefully crafted instruction on decoding and comprehension strategies is fundamental. The standards also note that students should read multiple genres and text types, both digital and print. We can't imagine any literacy educator disagreeing with either of these parts of the goal. While everyone agrees that teachers shouldn't just hand students hard texts and wish them well, the practice of scaffolded instruction is receiving renewed attention. How much is too much? When is it not enough? There is a deep body of research (e.g., Vygotsky, 1978; Wood, Bruner, & Ross, 1976; Wood & Wood, 1996) on the importance of scaffolding in instruction.

While everyone agrees that we shouldn't just hand students hard texts and wish them well, the practice of scaffolded instruction is receiving renewed attention. How much is too much? When is it not enough?

Scaffolded instruction is vital in reading instruction, and its practice is universal. Scaffolding in reading instruction occurs through the use of texts (Fountas & Pinnell, 2012), strategically deployed questions, prompts and cues (Frey & Fisher, 2010), and a gradient of instructional arrangements (Fisher & Frey, 2008; Pearson & Gallagher, 1983). Each of these dimensions of curriculum and instruction is essential for teaching students how to read and for building their capacity to read for meaning. For students to access complex text, their reading experiences must include a thoughtful progression of texts, scaffolds, and instructional arrangements.

A second dimension of the standards concerns exactly what students should be reading. The easy response is "grade-level texts, of course," but what exactly constitutes "grade level"? Teachers have operated under tacit agreements about grade level, often relying on local context and traditions. Haven't we all worked in schools where a particular title was considered the province of a specific grade level? For example, where we live, *Charlotte's Web* is third grade, and *Romeo and Juliet* is ninth grade. However, in many cases, these traditions seemed to be justified primarily because units and materials had already been developed and shifting the book to another grade was too much trouble. Given the gap between students' reading levels when they complete high school and the expectations for them when they attend college, the level of text complexity has increased. Teachers must use complex texts that continually stretch students' capacity to read and comprehend literary and informational texts. In other words, the expectation is that students will read and understand more complex texts than they have been expected to in the past. But to what end—and how do we know what makes a text complex?

▶ A New Definition of Text Complexity

In the past, text complexity and readability were viewed interchangeably by many practitioners, even as researchers cautioned otherwise (Hiebert, 2009). Readability has been estimated based on the average length of sentences, the number of syllables in sentences, and—in some cases—occurrences of rare words. These measures provided teachers with general information about readability and were used to gauge appropriate materials for students. But many have voiced concern that these measures missed the nuances present in many texts, often reporting readings as being easier than they really were. Works by Ernest Hemingway, for example, have been assigned a difficulty level ranging from grades 4 to 8, yet any teacher who has used his works of literature knows that the concepts, dialogue, and background knowledge needed by the reader make these texts far more complex than can be measured by a readability formula alone.

Modern definitions of text complexity extend beyond the numeric scores for texts and have been expanded to include qualitative evaluations as well as careful consideration of the reader and tasks. Fisher, Frey, and Lapp (2016) describe three aspects of text complexity, including:

- **Quantitative aspects,** which include formal readability measures typically conducted by computers
- **Qualitative aspects,** which include levels of meaning, structure, language conventionality and clarity, and knowledge demands typically assessed by human readers
- **Readers and tasks considerations,** which include a range of reader variables such as motivation, knowledge, and experiences and task design considerations such as purpose and levels of support provided.

Text analysis must always keep all three elements in mind.

Quantitative Evaluation

The temptation is to rely on the quantitative measures alone, which are derived from algorithms that yield numerical data; these measures can be calculated by a computer and do an adequate job of tentatively placing a text within a grade band. But these measures alone are inadequate for understanding why one piece of text is qualitatively more difficult

Video 1.1

Doug discusses text complexity.
resources.corwin.com/ rigorousreadingtx

To read a QR code, you must have a smartphone or tablet with a camera. We recommend that you download a QR code reader app that is made specifically for your phone or tablet brand.

than another with the same quantitative score. It is simply insufficient to use readability data (sentence length, use of rare words, and such) and assume that this is the only information needed for gauging text complexity. Furthermore, you can't derive much guidance in terms of your teaching points from quantitative analysis alone. The art of making meaningful qualitative evaluations is best left to the judgment of a knowledgeable educator who is deeply familiar with the texts in question.

For students to access complex text, their reading experiences must include a thoughtful progression of texts, scaffolds, and instructional arrangements.

Yet teachers should be able to use the quantitative tools that are available to create a list of potential texts that they might want to use. We are not suggesting that teachers only use texts that fit within the quantitative band for their grade level, but we are concerned that there are students who are never taught to read with texts that are of an appropriate grade-level challenge. Figure 1.1 provides current readability information for a range of tools.

Qualitative Evaluation

Qualitative evaluation requires considering a text across four dimensions: levels of meaning and purpose, structure, language convention and clarity, and knowledge demands (see Figure 1.2). Note that these descriptors mirror the teaching points we rely on during instruction. A given text is going to be variously more or less difficult within each of these areas, and it is unlikely that any text would be uniformly difficult across all four. Structure refers to the genre of the text, its organization and narration, the number of text features, and its use of graphics (if applicable). The *Magic School Bus* series of science stories, for instance, is made more accessible because it uses a narrative structure of a group of children and their teacher on field trips to explain complex topics. On the other hand, *Night* (Wiesel, 1982) uses a difficult structure—flashback—that can confuse readers.

A second dimension of qualitative measures of text complexity concerns levels of meaning. Some texts are straightforward in their presentation of information, while others use figurative language, or present dense and complex ideas. For example, the informational picture book *How Artists See Families* (Carroll, 1997) is less complex in terms of levels of meaning, as it explains each image in concrete and observable terms. While quantitatively easier, the picture book *Frida* (Winter, 2002), with its ambiguous and unexplained images reminiscent of Frida Kahlo's work, requires readers to understand the story on two levels.

Figure 1.1   Quantitative Text Complexity Grade Bands

Grade Band	Flesch-Kincaid	ATOS	DRP	TextEvaluator	Lexile
K–1	N/A	Grade 1: 1.6–3.3	N/A	N/A	N/A
2–3	1.98–5.34	2.8–5.1	42–54	100–590	450–790
4–5	4.51–7.73	5.0–7.0	52–60	405–730	770–980
6–8	6.51–10.34	7.0–10.0	57–67	550–940	955–1,155
9–10	8.32–12.12	9.7–12.0	62–72	750–1,125	1,080–1,305
11–12	10.34–14.2	11.2–14.1	67–74	890–1,360	1,215–1,355

Figure 1.2   Qualitative Factors of Text Complexity

Component	Aspects	When a NARRATIVE text is complex . . .	When an INFORMATIONAL text is complex . . .
Levels of Meaning and Purpose	• Density and complexity	Many ideas come at the reader, or there are multiple levels of meaning, some of which are not clearly stated.	Significant density and complexity, with multiple layers of content topics, are present. The reader is expected to critique or evaluate information.
	• Figurative language (narrative especially) • Analogies and abstract comparisons	There are many literary devices (e.g., metaphors, personification) or devices that the reader is not familiar with (e.g., symbolism, irony) as well as idioms or clichés.	The metaphors and analogies used are more abstract and require sophistication and depth of knowledge from the reader. The process or phenomenon used to make a comparison itself requires prior knowledge.
	• Purpose	Either the purpose is not stated or is intentionally withheld. The reader has to determine the theme or message.	The text may involve multiple purposes, some of which may be implicit; it requires the reader to critically analyze across texts to discern implicit purposes.

(Continued)

Figure 1.2 (Continued)

Component	Aspects	When a NARRATIVE text is complex . . .	When an INFORMATIONAL text is complex . . .
Structure	• Genre	The genre is unfamiliar or the author bends and expands the rules of the genre.	The text is presented as a specific genre but includes other embedded genres.
	• Organization	Organization distorts time or sequence in a deliberate effort to delay the reader's full understanding of the plot, process, or set of concepts; may include significant flashbacks, foreshadowing, or shifting perspectives.	The text may include a variety of conventional organizational patterns, which are dictated by text content, but with little notification or guidance to the reader.
	• Narration	Unreliable narrator provides a distorted or limited view to the reader; the reader must use other clues to deduce the truth; multiple narrators provide conflicting information; shifting points of view keep the reader guessing.	Less commonly a source of complexity, but the text could include narration within an informational structure, which could result in narration providing conflicting information; shifting points of view keep the reader guessing.
	• Text features	Fewer signposts such as headings, bold words, margin notes, font changes, or footnotes are used.	The text contains access features that require the reader to integrate extratextual information, such as preface/prologue, afterword/epilogue, and author/illustrator notes.
	• Graphics	Visual information is not repeated in the text itself, but the graphics or illustrations are essential to understanding the main ideas.	The text contains graphic elements that are less familiar to students and require interpretation, such as cross-sections, cutaways, and range and flow maps. Graphic elements have information that complements and is integrated with text.

Component	Aspects	When a NARRATIVE text is complex . . .	When an INFORMATIONAL text is complex . . .
Language Conventionality and Clarity	• Standard English and variations	Variations of standard English, such as regional dialects or vernaculars that the reader is not familiar with, are included.	The text uses language conventions and structures unfamiliar to the student, especially those that reflect voices found in specific content areas.
	• Register and voice	It is archaic, formal, scholarly, or fixed in time.	The register is domain-specific, formal, and/or scholarly.

Strong authoritative voice dominates the text. Text language is used to impart knowledge to the reader and makes little effort to engage the reader on a personal level. |
Knowledge Demands	• Background knowledge	The text places demands on the reader that extend far beyond one's experiences and provides little in the way of explanation of these divergent experiences.	The content demands specialized knowledge beyond the primary and secondary experiences of the reader and provides no bridge or scaffolding between known and unknown.
	• Prior knowledge	Specialized or technical content knowledge is presumed, and little in the way of review or explanation of these concepts is present in the text. The expectations extend beyond what the student has been taught in school.	Specialized or technical content knowledge is presumed; little review or explanation of these concepts is present in the text.
	• Cultural knowledge	The demands on the reader extend well beyond his or her cultural experiences and may include references to archaic or historical cultures.	The demands on the reader extend well beyond his or her cultural experiences and may include references to archaic or historical cultures.
	• Vocabulary	The words used are representations of complex ideas that are unfamiliar to the reader, or they are domain specific and not easily understood using context clues or morphological knowledge.	The vocabulary demand is extensive, domain specific, and representative of complex ideas; little is offered in the way of context clues.

The degree to which the language conventions are similar to or different from those commonly understood can also affect complexity. Hesse's use of font size and sentence grammar variants to represent her protagonist's cognitive processes in *Music of the Dolphins* (1996) conveys the story's message of a growing awareness and then rejection of human ways by a girl raised by dolphins. By comparison, *The Grouchy Ladybug* (Carle, 1996) carries the same quantitative measure (a Lexile score of 560) but tells a far simpler story using familiar language conventions.

Finally, the relative knowledge demanded of the reader plays into the level of complexity of a given text. Doug's difficulty with *Antigone* stemmed from the fact that it requires the reader to have a vast amount of cultural knowledge, in this case of ancient Greek mythology, to make sense of the text. By comparison, *Dateline: Troy* (Fleischman, 2006) recounts portions of the *Iliad* by comparing it to modern news and gossip stories. In this way, elements of the Trojan War are made familiar by comparing them to 20th century wars. Both texts feature major archetypes in literature, but whereas the first requires the reader to recognize them, the second assumes that the reader doesn't already know them and instead draws attention to them more overtly.

Matching Readers With Texts and Tasks

Quantitative and qualitative dimensions are solely about the characteristics of the text itself. The third facet in determining text complexity, however, is about the match between reader, text, and task. This last facet is where teaching lies, and in fact is the central theme of this book. We will return to this throughout these chapters, but for now, we want to consider the interaction between the reader and the text. There are myriad books to select from (over 304,912 new titles published in the U.S. in 2013), but only a few will make their way to your classroom or school. This aspect of text complexity ensures that teachers consider their students, the students sitting in front of them, when they select reading materials. That does not mean that students are limited to texts that they can already read, but it does mean that teachers have discretion in selecting texts that they believe will help their students grow as readers. As we will explore throughout this book, there are times when students read less complex texts and times when they read more complex texts. In reality, text complexity is a balancing act between providing sufficient opportunities for students to struggle and enough practice for them to develop habits. Teachers should consider the following when they select texts for students to read:

- provide students with examples of quality writing that mentor them as writers themselves;
- grant students access to excellent illustrations;
- allow students to see themselves—their religion, ethnicity, language, and culture—in the selected texts;
- permit students to interact—through the act of reading—with people who have different experiences and beliefs;
- depict a variety of family structures;
- offer a balanced portrayal of gender identities and roles in terms of the depiction of the characters and what the characters do; and
- interrupt gender, racial, or ability stereotypes.

Another way to find quality books is to review titles that have received national and international recognition. For example, the American Library Association awards the Newbery (for writing) and the Caldecott (for illustration) each year for the best children's books. The same organization presents the Coretta Scott King award to outstanding African American authors and illustrators of books for children and young adults. The University of Texas offers the Tomás Rivera award to for children's books that depict the Mexican American experience. The Orbus Pictus award is given by the National Council of Teachers of English for outstanding nonfiction written for children. The Hans Christian Andersen medal is presented biennially by the International Board of Books for Young People in recognition of the body of work of an author and of an illustrator. Each state awards a series of young reader medals for books that are particularly popular with students in the state. The state reading association or library association will have a list of these awards by year. In addition, the International Reading Association created the Children's Choice, Teen Choice, and Teachers' Choices awards.

Understanding the quantitative and qualitative properties of texts is essential, as are the considerations regarding the interaction between the reader and the text. While these are helpful categories, they do not provide instructional guidance for teachers hoping to build their students' comprehension of the texts. What do we do with complex texts once we have them? It's important to remember that there is no evidence that students can independently learn from books they can't read (Allington, 2002). When it comes to reading challenging texts, students must be adequately supported to unlock the meanings hidden within.

When it comes to reading challenging texts, students must be adequately supported to unlock the meanings hidden within.

▶ Reading Closely and Carefully

The intent of close reading is to foster critical thinking skills to deepen comprehension, a key aspect of the Texas Standards.

Selecting a text is more than simply choosing a title from a list or a bookshelf. We have developed a decision pathway to help teachers select texts for their students (see Figure 1.3). Sometimes, the text is great and might be useful. In those cases, consider path 1 and ask yourself if the text meets your instructional purpose, learning intention, or objective. Continue through the questions in path 1 to determine if the text is an appropriate choice. Other times, students need instruction in some aspect of reading. For example, if a group of fifth graders needed additional instruction to "make, correct, or confirm predictions using text features, characteristics of genre, and structures," the selected text would need to provide that opportunity and the teacher would follow path 2. Finally, students may need to build their knowledge base, especially if they are going to be able to read more widely about a topic. In that case, the teacher would select path 3 and consider the questions in that column before deciding on a specific text.

Much attention has been given to the process of close reading, which relies on repeated readings of short passages of complex texts. A key purpose of close reading is to encourage students to examine in detail what the text has to say. The first assumption behind the practice of close reading is that the text is worthy; not everything we read requires this kind of inspection. However, understanding the text itself is necessary for comprehension and is key to making the kind of analytic and evaluative judgments that mark a competent reader. One question we often hear is in regard to the use of close reading practices with students who are not yet fully independent readers. It is helpful to keep in mind that the intent of close reading is to foster critical thinking skills to deepen comprehension, a key aspect of the Texas Standards. Therefore, the thinking skills needed for close reading should begin in kindergarten. Although the delivery of the lesson is somewhat different when working with emergent readers, the intention is the same. The use of close reading in primary grades will be discussed in greater detail in Chapter 3.

We apply the same reasoning when working with students with disabilities. It is essential that they receive access to general curriculum, as stated in both federal law and widely accepted best practices. Our experiences have shown us that close reading is especially useful for these and other students for whom a "one and done" reading of a text is not sufficient. Close reading

Video 1.3

Doug discusses close reading.

resources.corwin.com/ rigorousreadingtx

Figure 1.3 Decision Pathways for Selecting Texts

Path 1 It's a Fantastic Text . . .	Path 2 My Students Need Reading Instruction About . . .	Path 3 I Want to Build My Students' Knowledge About . . .
What are my learning intentions?	What are my learning intentions?	What are my learning intentions?
Text Consideration: What are the qualitative and quantitative characteristics of the proposed text?	**Reader Consideration:** What are the reader's (or readers') cognitive capabilities, motivation, knowledge, and experiences?	**Reader Consideration:** What are the reader's (or readers') cognitive capabilities, motivation, knowledge, and experiences?
Reader Consideration: What are the reader's (or readers') cognitive capabilities, motivation, knowledge, and experiences?	**Text Consideration:** What are the qualitative and quantitative characteristics of the proposed text?	**Text Consideration:** What are the qualitative and quantitative characteristics of the proposed text?
Gap Analysis: What gap exists between the reader and the text I am considering?	**Gap Analysis:** What gap exists between the reader and the text I am considering?	**Gap Analysis:** What gap exists between the reader and the text I am considering?
Task Consideration: What instructional arrangement will best address this gap (teacher-led, peer-led, or independent)?	**Task Consideration:** What instructional arrangement will best address this gap (teacher-led, peer-led, or independent)?	**Task Consideration:** What instructional arrangement will best address this gap (teacher-led, peer-led, or independent)?
Text–Task Suitability: Does the proposed text align with the proposed task?	**Text–Task Suitability:** Does the proposed text align with the proposed task?	**Text–Task Suitability:** Does the proposed text align with the proposed task?
If **yes**, finalize decision and monitor progress toward identified learning intentions. If **no**, return to task consideration.	If **yes**, finalize decision and monitor progress toward learning intentions. If **no**, return to text consideration.	If **yes**, finalize decision and monitor progress toward learning intentions. If **no**, return to text and task considerations.

Source: Fisher, D., Frey, N., & Lapp, D. (2016). *Text complexity: Stretching readers with texts and tasks.* Thousand Oaks, CA: Corwin.

affords students with the gift of time to linger with a piece of text. While we have known for decades that multiple readings are essential for deep understanding, in practice, teachers have rarely afforded students with the time to do so. Some of the greatest gains we have witnessed in our own classrooms have been with students who have otherwise struggled as readers.

There has been debate about the role of activating prior knowledge in a close reading. Reading comprehension is not a skill that exists in a vacuum between the reader and the text immediately in front of her; it also hinges on the accumulation of the many texts and experiences that she has been exposed to throughout her lifetime (e.g., Rosenblatt, 2003). Therefore, a competent reader links her prior knowledge to the new information she is experiencing. We believe that thoughtful reading teachers must encourage students to analyze, make judgments, synthesize across multiple sources of information, formulate opinions, and create new products. To do this, they should be integrating what they have learned from the text with their prior knowledge and experiences. But we share the concern that, in too many cases, the rush to engage students in these critical thinking skills has meant that relatively little time is allocated for eyes on the text. Instead, after extensive pre-teaching of the content of the text by the teacher, the text is all too often given a quick once over. In these cases, true integration doesn't take place; instead, students are mostly drawing on what they already know. It's hard to make forward progress when you're mostly just treading water.

Reading comprehension is not a skill that exists in a vacuum between the reader and the text immediately in front of her; it also hinges on the accumulation of texts and experiences that she has been exposed to.

If students are going to access complex texts, they must been given the time to read and reread, to respond to questions that encourage them to return to the text, and to discuss their ideas in the company of others. A strong textual foundation also makes it possible for them to engage in critical thinking skills. It's analogous to a ladder: It doesn't matter how tall the ladder is if the lower rungs are not solid. In our own classrooms, we are witnessing what is happening with our students who struggle to read. We are finding that spending more time on the textual foundations—the lower rungs of the ladder—is making it possible for them to analyze, evaluate, and create.

Developing readers must apprentice to the kinds of problem-solving strategies that expert readers use when their comprehension breaks down. In part, this occurs when their teachers model, as we will discuss in the next chapter. But students also need to practice what they have been taught. When it comes to using complex text, teachers should expect comprehension to break down regularly, and they should seize the opportunities these breakdowns present. These are ideal for showing students how problem-solving comprehension strategies are summoned so that, over time, they become a part of their repertoire as skilled readers (Afflerbach, Pearson, & Paris, 2008). Simply said, this is how students will develop the reading and thinking skills required in the Texas standards. Consider, as an example, the grade 3 expectation that students "evaluate details read to determine key ideas." If the texts lack complexity, the key ideas and details will be obvious and students will not make errors; thus, no learning can occur. By using complex texts, in this case a text that has key ideas that are less obvious, students can learn to notice the details that eventually allow them to uncover the information. Will they get it right the first time? Probably not. They need instruction, including the access points that we describe in this book.

▶ The Importance of Comprehension Strategies Instruction for Accessing Complex Texts

The lights are out in Ms. Butler's fourth-grade classroom. Every eye is glued to the screen on which she has projected a website explaining the history of chocolate. She knows that the text is complex, as she had analyzed it earlier using the qualitative rubric, which is available for download on the companion website at resources.corwin.com/rigorousreadingtx. She identified that the prior knowledge needed, as well as the extensive use of metaphors (a function of figurative language) were especially challenging. She paired this information about the qualitative elements of the text with her knowledge of her students as readers. She had previously noticed that her students were not creating mental images as they read, a key Texas standard, and this has compromised their understanding of the texts they were reading. She decided to model this cognitive strategy for her students using a think-aloud and then asking them to apply their learning in small groups.

Ms. Butler reads the informational text aloud, pausing periodically to share her thinking about the text. At one point, she pauses and says,

> I see huge vats of chocolate melting and some guy
> standing there stirring the chocolate. I can just smell the
> sweetness of the chocolate as it melts. I'm picturing this
> in my mind so that I can create a mental image that will
> help me connect the information that the author wants
> me to remember.

These words are not in the text. Ms. Butler is describing her own mental visualizations so that her students will begin to do so on their own.

As she finishes the shared reading, having focused on the role chocolate has played in civilization and on visualization as a comprehension strategy, a group of students joins her for scaffolded reading instruction. All of the other students are engaged in collaborative conversations and peer learning activities. Ms. Butler knows that the students in this first group have significant difficulty with visualizing the text. She has selected an excerpt of *Charlie and the Chocolate Factory* by Roald Dahl (1964) to read with them. She knows that many of the students in this group have either read this book or will read this book after this lesson. However, that isn't her focus with them. The part of the book she has selected finds the group inside the chocolate factory looking at the chocolate river. She shares the passage with the group and asks each student to visualize as she reads. When she has finished, she asks for students to volunteer to share "the pictures in your minds."

Arturo volunteers to speak first and says, "I was looking down into the river, but I couldn't see anything because the chocolate was too thick." Sarah says, "The smell, ohh, that smell. I just can't stand it! It's too sweet. Who could eat that much chocolate?" Bryan adds, "I can feel it between my toes. It's almost like mud, but thicker. I try to splash the river with my feet, but the chocolate is so thick that it just moves around."

Ms. Butler reads other passages about chocolate that she has identified from the book. Again, students share their visualizations. After about 20 minutes, she is satisfied with their progress and excuses the members of this group to the collaborative learning activities and invites another group of students to the table.

The Texas Standards explicitly call for comprehension strategy instruction. This requires that teachers model and guide students such that they develop a habit of automatically using these strategies.

The Texas Standards explicitly call for comprehension strategy instruction. This requires that teachers model and guide students such that they develop a habit of automatically using these cognitive strategies. The problem in the past has been that the development of comprehension strategies has been seen as an outcome in and of itself. Today, comprehension strategies are viewed as a path toward understanding and accessing complex texts.

Comprehension strategies are taught to students of all developmental levels so that they may use them as tools to support their own understanding of a given text (e.g., Fisher, Lapp, & Frey, 2011). As with tools in a toolbox, the key to the usefulness of these strategies lies in how thoughtfully they are applied to suit a particular purpose. These strategies include the following:

- **Purpose-setting strategies** that allow students to explore the range of reasons for which they are reading. They may need to find information, answer a question,

Video 1.4

Teacher uses questioning techniques to aid student comprehension.
resources.corwin.com/ rigorousreadingtx

understand another culture or their own, enjoy the time, or develop an argument. Authors generally write for one of four basic reasons: to inform or explain; to entertain; to persuade or convince; or to enlighten or reveal a truth.

- **Questioning strategies** to predict and anticipate what might occur next in the text, to solve problems, and to clarify textual understanding
- **Summarizing strategies** to identify important information and accurately recount a text
- **Inferencing strategies** to "read between the lines" to identify clues in the text
- **Self-monitoring strategies** to determine when readers understand what they have read and notice when they have not
- **Connection strategies** to integrate what a reader has experienced and has learned with the information being read
- **Analysis strategies** to identify literary devices, determine the author's purpose, and evaluate texts

We believe there is a danger in teaching comprehension strategies in isolation of one another, which was a mistake commonly made in the past. Pinnell and Fountas (2003) remind us that

> [t]hese strategies are not linear in that first you engage one then another. In fact, reducing complex systems to a list . . . probably oversimplifies reading. *Teaching* strategies one at a time and telling students to consciously employ them, *one at a time,* may actually interfere with deep comprehension and make reading a meaningless exercise. (pp. 7–8)

Complex text instruction is an ideal opportunity to consolidate the many skills and strategies students are learning throughout their reading day. They locate information in the text, integrate it with their prior knowledge, and get to use comprehension strategies in real time to get themselves unstuck when understanding breaks down. The ability to coordinate all of these cognitive and metacognitive processes is not easy and requires a framework for instruction that doesn't leave students floundering alone.

Complex text instruction is an ideal opportunity to consolidate skills and strategies students are learning. They locate information in the text, integrate it with prior knowledge, and use comprehension strategies in real time.

Video 1.5

Teacher modeling comprehension strategies.
resources.corwin.com/ rigorousreadingtx

▶ Accessing Complex Texts Through a Gradual Release of Responsibility

Video 1.6

Doug talks about the gradual release of responsibility.

resources.corwin.com/ rigorousreadingtx

For students to access complex texts, they need intentional instruction that provides them with *access* to deep comprehension. In this book, we've identified five "access points," that is, five ways to intentionally guide students' comprehension of complex text. The framework that allows for the implementation of this type of intentional instruction is known as *gradual release of responsibility* (e.g., Fisher & Frey, 2008; Pearson & Fielding, 1991).

Our interpretation of the gradual-release-of-responsibility model includes the following five phases. Importantly, these are not presented in a prescriptive order. Rather, they can be combined, and teachers can start anywhere. For example, a group of students might enter the classroom and be asked to complete a journal entry about the text the class is reading (independent) and then be invited to share their thinking with a peer (collaborative) while the teacher listens in to identify gaps in understanding so that she can model her thinking and then set the learning intention for the day. She could also identify gaps in understanding for her guided instruction and following her modeling, students may be asked to work independently or collaboratively again. The five components we look for in a lesson designed around the gradual-release-of-responsibility framework include:

- *Learning intentions*: Students are informed early on about the learning intentions. Teachers identify specific content goals based on grade-level standards and communicate the expected learning outcomes to students. Also, given the number of English language learners and standard English learners, teachers analyze the content to determine to students as well. Further, teachers identify the social aspects of learning and communicate those expectations to students. The evidence for this component was summarized by Marzano, Pickering, and Pollock (2002) and Hill and Flynn (2006).
- *Modeling*: Students are provided an example of the thinking required to complete each task. The teacher, not other students, shares his or her thinking while

reading such that students get a glimpse inside the mind of an expert. As Duffy (2014) pointed out, "The only way to model thinking is to talk about how to do it. That is, we provide a verbal description of the thinking one does or, more accurately, an *approximation* of the thinking involved" (p. 11).

- *Guided instruction*: Through the strategic use of prompts, cues, and questions, teachers transfer some of the responsibility for learning to students. Typically, this occurs in needs-based groups of three to six students who have been purposefully selected based on formative assessment data (Avalos, Plasencia, Chavez, & Rascón, 2007/2008). Guided instruction can also occur with the whole class or with individual students as teachers address errors without telling students the answers.

- *Collaborative learning*: Students complete collaborative learning activities designed to provide them opportunities to use language and explore the content. The tasks must be structured to build on students' knowledge and be differentiated so as to not cause stress for students who currently perform below grade level (Matthews & Kesner, 2003). As we will see in the chapter on collaborative learning, some tasks include individual accountability as part of the group interaction (Johnson, Johnson, & Holubec, 2008), which allows teachers to check for understanding.

- *Independent learning*: As part of the gradual release of responsibility, students must apply what they have learned, especially in new situations or contexts (Harvey & Chickie-Wolf, 2007). Although independent learning is the goal of education, students are often assigned independent tasks for which they do not yet have the skills to complete alone. Some tasks, such as independent reading, writing prompts, and journaling, can occur in the classroom. Others, especially spiral review tasks, can

For students to access complex texts, they need intentional instruction that provides them with access to deep comprehension.

be completed outside of the school day, either in an after-school program or at home.

In the remainder of this book, we describe in detail each access point, always through the lens of complex texts. The chapters are as

Although independent learning is the goal of education, students are often assigned independent tasks for which they do not yet have the skills to complete alone.

- Chapter 2, "Access Point One: Modeling and Learning Intentions," Learning intentions describes the first access point—establishing the expectations or objectives of the lesson, or the learning target— and explains the ways that teachers can model their critical thinking for students as they read. In this chapter, we discuss the use of think-alouds and interactive shared readings, with special attention on the modeling of annotation skills.
- Chapter 3, "Access Point Two: Close and Scaffolded Reading Instruction," describes the second access point: close reading and scaffolded reading instruction. The practice of close reading, which emphasizes repeated readings, discussion, and critical thinking, requires scaffolded instruction. Text-dependent questions, prompts, and cues form the basis of these scaffolds and provide students with the teacher-supported experiences they need to read increasingly complex texts.
- Chapter 4, "Access Point Three: Collaborative Conversations," describes the third access point: collaborative conversations. These peer-led learning experiences require tasks that encourage students to interact and to apply what they have learned through close reading to develop deeper understandings of complex texts. In this chapter, we discuss a number of ways that teachers can facilitate student-to-student collaboration, including literature circles, discussion roundtables, reciprocal teaching, and collaborative strategic reading.
- Chapter 5, "Access Point Four: An Independent Reading Staircase," focuses on students' ability to

climb the figurative reading staircase as they apply what they have learned and read increasingly complex texts independently. While they may be reading individually, they are not reading alone, and well-designed instruction is essential in this phase. This chapter explains how to craft this instruction through the use of texts that build background knowledge and through peer-conferencing strategies that foster metacognitive awareness.

- Chapter 6, "Access Point Five: Assessing Students' Understanding," concerns itself with demonstrating understanding and assessing performance. These practices are not only for the teacher to use when measuring mastery but also for students to use to propel future learning. This chapter focuses on what occurs after reading, including feedback and assessment.

The intention behind effective instruction is for students to expand their capacity to deeply understand these kinds of complex texts outside the company of their teachers. It is this understanding that lies at the heart of college and career readiness.

Doug's and Nancy's teachers that you met in the opening of this chapter, however well meaning, didn't know how to use these access points. Doug's teacher released cognitive responsibility much too suddenly, and he was left to try to find an outside source of information because he didn't know how to locate it within the text. Nancy's teacher never released any of the responsibility and did too much of the cognitive heavy lifting for her students. The teacher's assessments focused on the wrong measures, and she never did figure out that Nancy hadn't read the book. In using a range of access points, teachers can avoid these all-too-common pitfalls and balance support with challenge.

▶ Summary

One method for measuring text complexity is quantitative and relies on the number and types of words in the text; this measure is useful for situating a text within a grade band. However, this method of measurement does not uncover the qualitative values that render a text more or less complex. These include levels of meaning and purpose, structure, language conventions and clarity, and knowledge demands. These values give us insight into *what* to teach. The third facet of complexity concerns the reader characteristics and task demands, which inform *how* we teach complex texts. As students read these texts closely, they need support and instruction on how to identify textual elements and mine texts for understanding, as well as on how to use comprehension strategies to repair meaning when it becomes muddled. The intention behind effective instruction is for students to expand their capacity to deeply understand these kinds of complex texts outside the company of their teachers. It is this understanding that lies at the heart of college and career readiness. By equipping students to take on an ever-widening range of texts, we afford them their independence and extend their understanding of and influence on the biological, social, and physical world around them.

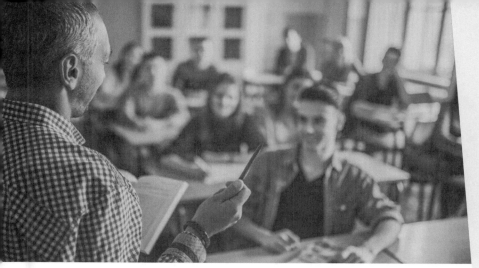

istock.com/skynesher

Access Point One

Modeling and Learning Intentions

Ms. Carver asks her students to get out their copies of *Number the Stars* (Lowry, 1989) while she places her copy of the book on the document camera. "Scholars," she begins,

> Today we're going to notice the specific words that the
> author has chosen and practice asking questions while
> we read. I'm going to share some of my thinking with
> you, especially about the author's words and the questions
> I have when I am reading. I'll give you a chance to try it
> with your reading partner.

After leading a discussion of the plot thus far, she begins to read while students follow silently in their books (her thinking aloud is italicized).

> "Your names?" the officer barked.

"Annemarie Johansen. And this is my sister—"

"Quiet! Let her speak for herself. Your name?" He was glaring at Ellen. *"Barked" and "glaring" are words the author is using to help me imagine this Nazi officer's anger. The author's word choice is important and in this case helps me think about the seriousness of the situation.*

Ellen swallowed. "Lise," she said, and cleared her throat. "Lise Johansen." *I know why she's lying. She doesn't want them to know she's Jewish so she pretends to be a member of the family. I'll bet the Johansens will also lie for Ellen.*

The officer stared at them grimly. "Now," Mama said in a strong voice, "you have seen that we are not hiding anything. May my children go back to bed?" *I was right. That's just what Mrs. Johansen did.*

The officer ignored her. Suddenly he grabbed a handful of Ellen's hair. Ellen winced. *Why would he pull Ellen's hair? Does he suspect something?*

He laughed scornfully. "You have a blond child sleeping in the other room. And you have this blond daughter—" he gestured toward Annemarie with his head. "Where did you get the dark-haired one?" *Oh, no! What will the Johansens say? Now I understand why the title of this chapter is "Who Is the Dark-Haired One?"* (Lowry, 1989, pp. 46–47).

After discussing the content of the passage, Ms. Carver leads a discussion about the think-aloud. "What are the ways I helped myself to understand what was happening in the text?" she asks. Jerome offers, "You made predictions about what would happen next." Delia adds, "You asked questions, like when the Nazi pulled Ellen's hair." While students respond, Ms. Carver records their ideas on chart paper. When finished, the list reads,

- Analyze word choices
- Make predictions and confirmations
- Ask questions
- Make connections to the title
- Visualize
- Think about what we already know about a character

She asks students to listen to the next portion of the text and make suggestions about predictive statements and questions. She pauses after every few sentences to prompt suggestions and writes their ideas on a second piece of chart paper. They continue to practice as a class using the next few pages of text. After several cycles of modeling and scaffolding, she asks students to work in pairs; each student will read a page from the book to the other while using think-aloud statements to support their comprehension.

Accessing complex texts requires structured time for students to work through new strategies and practice skills. Of course, students should know what they are expected to learn. A number of studies have found that when the teacher states objectives and provides feedback, student learning increases (Hattie & Donoghue, 2016). However, while establishing purpose through learning intentions primes learning, it does not ensure that it will occur; priming is insufficient without further instruction. Simply telling students what they are to learn doesn't guarantee they will learn it. A second technique for helping students learn new concepts and skills includes modeling through demonstration, that is, stopping to emphasize the parts of a text that offer examples of the stated learning intentions. A planning template appears in Figure 2.1.

A number of studies have found that when the teacher states objectives and provides feedback, student learning increases.

There are a wide range of topics for which teachers can provide models. This book centers on the topic of complex texts. It is important to note that Ms. Carver did not select a text that her students could read independently or even one that they could read with a little assistance. She selected a complex text that required intentional instruction. As noted in the discussion about the lesson, there are places in a given complex text that require teacher modeling or thinking aloud. Other parts of the text might be approproriate for close readings, collaborative conversations, partner reading, or independent reading. Teachers must identify the appropriate task for the text. To ensure that students can access complex texts, their teachers must first select complex texts and then model their thinking about the text. This type of teaching requires active involvement and shared responsibility between teachers and their students.

▶ Accessing Complex Text Requires Modeling

As Wilhelm (2001) notes, "[T]eachers model their thinking by voicing all the things they are noticing, doing, seeing, feeling, and asking as they process the text" (p. 26). In other words, the idea is that the teacher explicitly

Figure 2.1 Planning Learning Intentions and Modeling

Assessed Need: I have noticed that the students in my classroom need to work on:

Standards:

Text I will use:

Materials needed for this lesson are:

Learning intentions for the lesson are:

Model

- Parts to emphasize

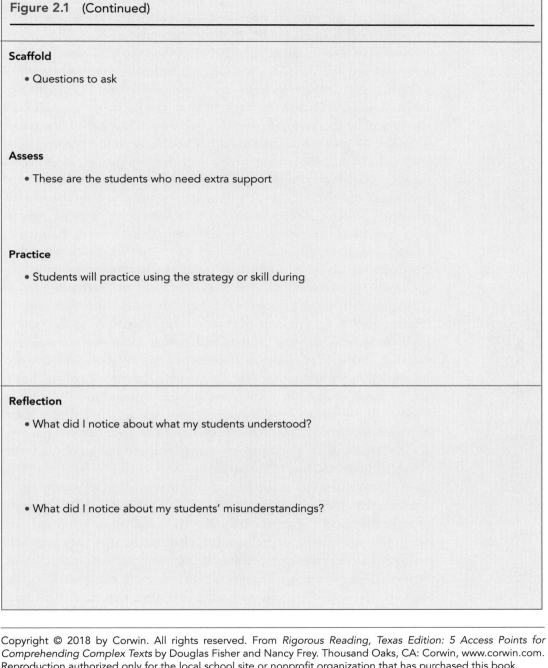

Figure 2.1 (Continued)

Scaffold

- Questions to ask

Assess

- These are the students who need extra support

Practice

- Students will practice using the strategy or skill during

Reflection

- What did I notice about what my students understood?

- What did I notice about my students' misunderstandings?

or intentionally models the strategies that readers can use as they read. Over time and with practice, students will develop habits based on the strategies that their teachers model. They will no longer need to stop reading to visualize or predict; rather, these behaviors will occur automatically. But as "knowledge and skills are obtained," students may need to be reintroduced to comprehension strategies and their application to more complex texts. All readers regularly fall back on strategies for resolving confusions when meaning breaks down. Once comprehension is regained, the reader continues. An important aspect of reading instruction is that teachers show students how and when to use these strategies when they get stuck. That's precisely why we don't want to excuse students who struggle to read from this kind of instruction. Arguably, they are the ones who can benefit the most from it. Because it is the teacher who is assuming most of the cognitive load during modeling, all students can access the text. To distance struggling students from this instruction is to magnify the difficulties they already possess. In other words, how would you learn to repair something if you were systematically excused every time someone began using a tool?

Video 2.1

A teacher models for her students.
resources.corwin.com/ rigorousreadingtx

Teachers can model any number of things that they want their students to learn, from how to interact with peers to how to compose an essay. In this book, we're addressing the topic of accessing complex text, so we will focus our discussion of modeling around the factors that contribute to text complexity. At the beginning of this chapter, Ms. Carver focused on knowledge demands (specifically vocabulary) and levels of meaning (specifically, density and complexity) as she modeled from *Number the Stars*. She knew these elements would factor into her students' comprehension of the text, and she used a think-aloud process to give voice to the ways she maintained her understanding of the passage.

We want students to recognize that complex texts require more from us as readers than those readings that are a more comfortable fit. Novice readers make the mistake of approaching all texts as equivalent, when they are not. In too many cases, when the text is challenging, they turn away and give up. As an expert reader, you activate different processes depending on the level of complexity you encounter. You know that you'll need to make notes for yourself when you're reading a James Joyce novel with your book club. You know how to look up an unfamiliar tax code in the manual that accompanied your annual tax return forms. When you encounter an unknown term while reading about the side effects listed in your prescription medicine insert, you consult several trusted resources. Novice readers don't automatically do these things.

Modeling is a time when you highlight the areas that you predict will be difficult for students, and you show them how you resolve comprehension problems. In addition, it is an important opportunity to show them how you interact with complex text.

Below, we will discuss three aspects of modeling and two methods for doing so:

- Model that which is difficult for students
- Model ways to resolve problems
- Model how you interact with text
- Model through think-alouds
- Model through interactive shared readings

Taken together, what you are really modeling are the habits of active readers when confronted with challenging text. You are modeling persistence and a willingness to stick with something more difficult because it's worth it.

Model That Which Is Difficult for Students

The first principle of modeling is that you are selective in what you model. There's not much point in modeling what students already know how to do, and in any case, it is not going to provide them with access to a complex text. Instead, analyze the text in advance for the four elements of text complexity (see Figure 1.2) and choose one or two aspects to highlight through your modeling.

When Mr. Jefferson's first-grade class was reading *The Three Little Wolves and the Big Bad Pig* (Trivizas, 1993), he knew that his students would not have difficulty with prior knowledge as they had been comparing folktales for several weeks. He also knew that his students would not have trouble understanding the genre, organization, or narration. However, the vocabulary demand was higher, with individual words such as *croquet, sledgehammer, concrete*, and *battledore and shuttlecock* likely to cause his students some confusion. In addition, he knew that he would have to model his thinking about the density of the text—especially focus on the change in roles—and the importance of the illustrations in conveying meaning.

At one point while modeling the text, Mr. Jefferson said,

> I want to reread this part because I think I'm getting
> confused. I think that the traditional story is getting in the
> way. The pig is the bad guy in this story because he's the one
> huffing and puffing and trying to blow the house down.

Novice readers make the mistake of approaching all texts as equivalent, when they are not. In too many cases, when the text is challenging, they turn away and give up.

Later in the text, Mr. Jefferson said,

> I'm not sure that I've ever heard the phrase *battledore and shuttlecock* before. When I look at the picture, I see the wolves playing a game that looks like tennis, but there isn't a ball. It reminds me of badminton. It's a strange little thing that they're hitting back and forth. That must be the game that they're playing because the author says that they are playing *battledore and shuttlecock* in the garden when they see the big bad pig.

In addition, strand 2 of the Texas English Language Arts and Reading Standards provides clear expectations for students' comprehension strategy development (see Figure 2.2). Starting in Kindergarten, students:

(A) establish purpose for reading assigned and self-selected texts with adult assistance;

(B) generate questions about text before, during, and after reading to deepen understanding and gain information with adult assistance;

(C) make and confirm predictions using text features and structures with adult assistance;

(D) create mental images to deepen understanding with adult assistance;

(E) make connections to personal experiences, ideas in other texts, and society with adult assistance;

(F) make inferences and use evidence to support understanding with adult assistance;

(G) evaluate details to determine what is most important with adult assistance;

(H) synthesize information to create new understanding with adult assistance; and

(I) monitor comprehension and make adjustments such as rereading, using background knowledge, checking for visual cues, and asking questions when understanding breaks down with adult assistance.

Naturally, these expectations change and grow over the K–12 continuum. But our point is this. Teachers can use the expectations in strand 2 to identify the ways in which their students struggle and then model appropriate strategy use for their students, slowly developing students' habits with

Figure 2.2 Strand 2 Vertical Alignment of the Texas K–12 English Language Arts and Reading Standards

English Language Arts and Reading K – 12 Vertical Alignment

Strand 2

Comprehension skills: listening, speaking, reading, writing, and thinking using multiple texts. The student uses metacognitive skills to both develop and deepen comprehension of increasingly complex texts. The student is expected to:

Kindergarten 110.2	Grade 1 110.3	Grade 2 110.4	Grade 3 110.5	Grade 4 110.6	Grade 5 110.7	Grade 6 110.22	Grade 7 110.23	Grade 8 110.24	English I 110.36	English II 110.37	English III 110.38	English IV 110.39
(5)	(6)	(6)	(6)	(6)	(6)	(5)	(5)	(5)	(4)	(4)	(4)	(4)
(A) establish purpose for reading assigned and self-selected texts with adult assistance;	(A) establish purpose for reading assigned and self-selected texts with adult assistance;	(A) establish purpose for reading assigned and self-selected texts;	(A) establish purpose for reading assigned and self-selected texts;	(A) establish purpose for reading assigned and self-selected texts;	(A) establish purpose for reading assigned and self-selected texts;	(A) establish purpose for reading assigned and self-selected text;	(A) establish purpose for reading assigned and self-selected texts;	(A) establish purpose for reading assigned and self-selected texts;	(A) establish purpose for reading assigned and self-selected texts;	(A) establish purpose for reading assigned and self-selected texts;	(A) establish purpose for reading assigned and self-selected texts;	(A) establish purpose for reading assigned and self-selected texts;
(B) generate questions about text before, during, and after reading to deepen understanding and gain information with adult assistance;	(B) generate questions about text before, during, and after reading to deepen understanding and gain information with adult assistance;	(B) generate questions about text before, during, and after reading to deepen understanding and gain information;	(B) generate questions about text before, during, and after reading to deepen understanding and gain information;	(B) generate questions about text before, during, and after reading to deepen understanding and gain information;	(B) generate questions about text before, during, and after reading to deepen understanding and gain information;	(B) generate questions about text before, during, and after reading to deepen understanding and gain information;	(B) generate questions about text before, during, and after reading to deepen understanding and gain information;	(B) generate questions about text before, during, and after reading to deepen understanding and gain information;	(B) generate questions about text before, during, and after reading to deepen understanding and gain information	(B) generate questions about text before, during, and after reading to deepen understanding and gain information	(B) generate questions about text before, during, and after reading to deepen understanding and gain information	(B) generate questions about text before, during, and after reading to deepen understanding and gain information
(C) make and confirm predictions using text features and structures with adult assistance;	(C) make, correct, or confirm predictions using text features, characteristics of genre, and structures with adult assistance;	(C) make, correct, or confirm predictions using text features, characteristics of genre, and structures;	(C) make, correct, or confirm predictions using text features, characteristics of genre, and structures;	(C) make, correct, or confirm predictions using text features, characteristics of genre, and structures;	(C) make, correct, or confirm predictions using text features, characteristics of genre, and structures;	(C) make, correct, or confirm predictions using text features, characteristics of genre, and structures;	(C) make, correct, or confirm predictions using text features, characteristics of genre, and structures;	(C) make, correct, or confirm predictions using text features, characteristics of genre, and structures;	(C) make and correct or confirm predictions using text features, characteristics of genre, and structures;	(C) make and correct or confirm predictions using text features, characteristics of genre, and structures;	(C) make and correct or confirm predictions using text features, characteristics of genre, and structures;	(C) make and correct or confirm predictions using text features, characteristics of genre, and structures;
(D) create mental images to deepen understanding with adult assistance;	(D) create mental images to deepen understanding with adult assistance;	(D) create mental images to deepen understanding;	(D) create mental images to deepen understanding;	(D) create mental images to deepen understanding;	(D) create mental images to deepen understanding;	(D) create mental images to deepen understanding;	(D) create mental images to deepen understanding;	(D) create mental images to deepen understanding;	(D) create mental images to deepen understanding;	(D) create mental images to deepen understanding;	(D) create mental images to deepen understanding;	(D) create mental images to deepen understanding;
(E) make connections to personal experiences, ideas in other texts, and society with adult assistance;	(E) make connections to personal experiences, ideas in other texts, and society with adult assistance;	(E) make connections to personal experiences, ideas in other texts, and society;	(E) make connections to personal experiences, ideas in other texts, and society;	(E) make connections to personal experiences, ideas in other texts, and society;	(E) make connections to personal experiences, ideas in other texts, and society;	(E) make connections to personal experiences, ideas in other texts, and society;	(E) make connections to personal experiences, ideas in other texts, and society;	(E) make connections to personal experiences, ideas in other texts, and society;	(E) make connections to personal experiences, ideas in other texts, and society;	(E) make connections to personal experiences, ideas in other texts, and society;	(E) make connections to personal experiences, ideas in other texts, and society;	(E) make connections to personal experiences, ideas in other texts, and society;

Kindergarten - Grade 8, Adopted May 10, 2017
High School, English I IV, Adopted June 23, 2017

(Continued)

Figure 2.2 (Continued)

English Language Arts and Reading K – 12 Vertical Alignment

Strand 2

Kindergarten 110.2	Grade 1 110.3	Grade 2 110.4	Grade 3 110.5	Grade 4 110.6	Grade 5 110.7	Grade 6 110.22	Grade 7 110.23	Grade 8 110.24	English I 110.36	English II 110.37	English III 110.38	English IV 110.39
(5)	(6)	(6)	(6)	(6)	(6)	(5)	(5)	(5)	(4)	(4)	(4)	(4)
(F) make inferences and use evidence to support understanding with adult assistance;	(F) make inferences and use evidence to support understanding with adult assistance;	(F) make inferences and use evidence to support understanding;	(F) make inferences and use evidence to support understanding;	(F) make inferences and use evidence to support understanding;	(F) make inferences and use evidence to support understanding;	(F) make inferences and use evidence to support understanding;	(F) make inferences and use evidence to support understanding;	(F) make inferences and use evidence to support understanding;	(F) make inferences and use evidence to support understanding;	(F) make inferences and use evidence to support understanding;	(F) make inferences and use evidence to support understanding;	(F) make inferences and use evidence to support understanding;
(G) evaluate details to determine what is most important with adult assistance;	(G) evaluate details to determine what is most important with adult assistance;	(G) evaluate details read to determine key ideas;	(G) evaluate details read to determine key ideas;	(G) evaluate details read to determine key ideas;	(G) evaluate details read to determine key ideas;	(G) evaluate details read to determine key ideas;	(G) evaluate details read to determine key ideas;	(G) evaluate details read to determine key ideas;	(G) evaluate details read to determine key ideas;	(G) evaluate details read to determine key ideas;	(G) evaluate details read to understand key ideas;	(G) evaluate details read to analyze key ideas;
(H) synthesize information to create new understanding with adult assistance; and	(H) synthesize information to create new understanding with adult assistance; and	(H) synthesize information to create new understanding; and	(H) synthesize information to create new understanding; and	(H) synthesize information to create new understanding; and	(H) synthesize information to create new understanding; and	(H) synthesize information to create new understanding; and	(H) synthesize information to create new understanding; and	(H) synthesize information to create new understanding; and	(H) synthesize information from two texts to create new understanding; and	(H) synthesize information from multiple texts to create new understanding; and	(H) synthesize information from a variety of text types to create new understanding; and	(H) synthesize information from a variety of text types to create new understanding; and
(I) monitor comprehension and make adjustments such as re-reading, using background knowledge, checking for visual cues, and asking questions when understanding breaks down with adult assistance.	(I) monitor comprehension and make adjustments such as re-reading, using background knowledge, checking for visual cues, and asking questions when understanding breaks down.	(I) monitor comprehension and make adjustments such as re-reading, using background knowledge, checking for visual cues, and asking questions when understanding breaks down.	(I) monitor| comprehension and make adjustments such as re-reading, using background knowledge, asking questions, and annotating when understanding breaks down.	(I) monitor comprehension and make adjustments such as re-reading, using background knowledge, asking questions, and annotating when understanding breaks down.	(I) monitor comprehension and make adjustments such as re-reading, using background knowledge, asking questions, and annotating when understanding breaks down.	(I) monitor comprehension and make adjustments such as re-reading, using background knowledge, asking questions, and annotating when understanding breaks down.	(I) monitor comprehension and make adjustments such as re-reading, using background knowledge, asking questions, and annotating when understanding breaks down.	(I) monitor comprehension and make adjustments such as re-reading, using background knowledge, asking questions, and annotating when understanding breaks down.	(I) monitor comprehension and make adjustments such as re-reading, using background knowledge, asking questions, and annotating when understanding breaks down.	I) monitor comprehension and make adjustments such as re-reading, using background knowledge, asking questions, and annotating when understanding breaks down.	(I) monitor comprehension and make adjustments such as re-reading, using background knowledge, asking questions, annotating, and using outside sources when understanding breaks down.	(I) monitor comprehension and make adjustments such as re-reading, using background knowledge, asking questions, annotating, and using outside sources when understanding breaks down.

Kindergarten – Grade 8, Adopted May 10, 2017

High School, English I – IV, Adopted June 23, 2017

Source: Texas Education Agency. Used with permission.

these strategies. In doing so, students will be more successful when they are assessed formally on the STARR (and its successor) and when they are expected to read for their job or in college.

Model Ways to Resolve Problems

The second principle of modeling is that you model ways to resolve problems and confusions. Complex text by definition is going to challenge students' understanding across one or more of the four elements that contribute to the text complexity (see Figure 1.2). Modeling is an ideal time to show students how you get yourself going again when comprehension breaks down. Often, it is the vocabulary that interferes with understanding. It is impossible to try to directly teach all of the words students will encounter as they read. Instead, teachers must help students build habits related to word solving. Students should learn how to use context clues, word parts or morphology, and resources to uncover the meaning of unknown words. These three categories are worthy of attention during modeling.

Modeling is an ideal time to show students how you get yourself going again when comprehension breaks down. Teachers must help students build habits related to word solving.

Structural Analysis: Looking Inside Words

When readers come to an unknown word, one of the things that they can do is look inside the word to see if there are any clues to the word's meaning. Understanding morphology, including prefixes, suffixes, roots, bases, and cognates, helps the reader make an educated guess about an unknown word. For example, if the reader has never been exposed to the word *paleozoology*, she or he can make an educated guess about this field using knowledge about prefixes and suffixes. In fact, the word is fairly easy to figure out when you remember that *paleo* means old or ancient, *zoo* relates to animals, and *-ology* relates to the study of something.

But simply providing students with a morphology list is not likely to change their behavior when they come to unknown words. Instead, teachers need to model the use of morphology in understanding words. For example, while reading a sentence that contained the word *heterozygous*, the biology teacher modeled his use of morphology saying, "I know that *hetero* means different, so this must be the one that has two different alleles, or different versions, of a specific gene."

Of course, morphology does not always work, and students should be provided with examples that remind them to check other clues as well. Our favorite example of this occurred in an English as a Second Language classroom when the teacher got to the word *repeat*. She said,

Video 2.2

An elementary teacher models word solving.
resources.corwin.com/ rigorousreadingtx

I got this one. I know that *re-* means to do again. So I'm going to *peat* again. Wait, I have no idea what that means! I better check the context clues and look outside the word to see if I can figure this out.

Context Clues: Looking Outside Words

In addition to looking inside words, students have to be taught to look outside of words to figure out their meaning. This happens through an understanding of context clues. Although context clues are not infallible, they can be helpful. There are a number of different kinds of context clues, such as embedded synonyms, antonyms, direct definitions, and the use of punctuation. Again, students need to be taught how to use these tools. Modeling provides students with examples that can be built into habits.

For example, when reading about the "supermoon" predicted for January 2, 2018, the teacher noted the word *fatalities* in the news report. There had been quite a bit of news coverage around the world that this astronomical event, which brought the Moon into close range of the Earth, would cause widespread flooding and earthquakes. She made the connection between *fatalities* in the beginning of the sentence and the use of "the number dead" later in the sentence. Another example occurred when the teacher modeled using punctuation, in this case a dependent clause that contained additional and specific information about a more difficult word. Just as we discussed with word parts, teachers should model when the use of context clues fail.

Again, the goal is for students to develop a habit that they can use independently when they come across unknown words. Like most of the systems we use when reading and trying to make meaning, they don't always work. When these two systems—word parts and context clues—fail, it's time to look further outside the word and use resources.

Using Resources: Looking Further Outside Words

"When all else fails, look it up" is a common motto of teachers, and for good reason. When the systems we have for figuring out unknown words within a text do not help, it's time to turn our attention to the resources we have at our disposal. Once upon a time, that was limited to printed dictionaries and glossaries. Today, we have a plethora of resources at our fingertips because of the Internet. For example, the visual dictionary (http://visual.merriam-webster.com) is a great resource that students can be taught to use. The same holds for the many specialized dictionaries, such as the following:

In addition to looking inside words, students have to be taught to look outside of words to figure out their meaning. This happens through an understanding of context clues.

- **Science:** http://www.thesciencedictionary.com
- **History:** http://www.babylon.com/define/52/History-Dictionary.html
- **Mathematics:** http://www.amathsdictionaryforkids.com
- **Art:** http://www.artlex.com
- **Sports and fitness**: http://dictionary.babylon.com/sports

As with word parts and context clues, teachers should model their use of resources such as these and model the appropriate ways to ask other people for help. This can be as simple as calling a friend on the classroom phone or texting someone for more information.

Modeling word solving should be integrated with other approaches to understanding the text, such as those based on comprehension strategies and on using text structures and text features. We are not suggesting that teachers focus only on modeling word solving, but rather that they include word solving in their shared readings and think-alouds so that students have access to examples of expert thinking about words. It is important to emphasize that teachers should model their thinking, selecting the content of the modeling to coincide with the aspects of the text that contribute to their complexity. This is one of the keys to accessing complex texts. Modeling is not random, "whatever comes to mind," but rather purposeful instruction focused on specific identified aspects of text complexity.

Model How You Interact With Text

A third principle of modeling provides students with examples of how proficient readers act on text to support their comprehension. Complex text requires interaction with the text, yet many students approach texts rather passively. They don't know that they should be making notes to themselves, especially to guide their rereading. Annotation of text, the practice of making notes for oneself during reading, is an essential practice for closely reading complex text. As well, it is useful when writing about the text, as students consult their annotations to formulate arguments, analyze information, and make connections within and outside of the text. Importantly, these annotations have a life beyond their initial construction. They are used in discussions, and some teachers even collect the annotated texts for the purpose of assessment. Adler and Van Doren (1972) describe the most common annotation marks:

- **Underlining** for major points.
- **Vertical lines in the margin** to denote longer statements that are too long to be underlined.

- **Star, asterisk, or other doodad in the margin** to be used sparingly to emphasize the ten or dozen most important statements. You may want to fold a corner of each page where you make such a mark or place a slip of paper between the pages.
  - **Numbers in the margin** to indicate a sequence of points made by the author in development of an argument.
- **Numbers of other pages in the margin** to indicate where else in the book the author makes the same points.
- **Circling of key words or phrases** to serve much the same function as underlining.
- **Writing in the margin, or at the top or bottom of the page** to record questions (and perhaps answers) that a passage raises in your mind. (pp. 49–50)

These annotation methods are ideal for use during modeling, as they allow teachers to demonstrate the habits of an active reader. The types of annotations should be consistent with the developmental needs of students. For example, in the primary grades annotations might be confined to underlining key points and circling unfamiliar words. As students progress into the intermediate grades, teachers begin to add other marks to indicate surprise or highlight questions we may have. In our modeling of annotations, we make sure that we are also writing our observations or queries so we can consult them later. As students move into middle and high school, we add numeration of the author's arguments and claims.

Student annotation can be limited when students can't write directly on the text. We circumvent this in several ways. Sometimes we ask students to annotate on sticky notes they affix to the page. If the passage is a shorter one, we photocopy it on large paper and ask them to write in the broad margins. Some of our colleagues have developed forms to accompany a reading, and one of our colleagues asks her students to slip the text into a clear plastic protective sleeve to develop temporary annotations.

As we noted earlier, modeling with complex texts teaches students the importance of persistence when confronted with challenge. Mere exhortations to try harder are insufficient; what is modeled should be a first step in equipping students with the tools they need to resolve comprehension problems. In the next section, we will discuss two methods for modeling with complex texts: think-alouds and shared reading.

Model Through Think-Alouds

The ninth-grade earth science class is focused on live video streamed from a news agency showing the eruption of a small volcano located near the Eyjafjallajoekull glacier in Iceland. The voice of the teacher narrates what he is seeing as he watches with his class. "As I'm watching this, I'm thinking about how unique this eruption is," he says. "With most volcanoes, there are earthquakes that signal something might be happening. But these volcanoes around Iceland don't give any warning. I checked on the USGS website, and the tremors were really small." He continues, "I'm also noticing that the eruption is more like a fissure. See how it's tearing here?" he gestures. "It's awfully close to this glacier. If the fissure keeps widening, it's going to have an impact on the glacier itself." The teacher concludes, "I know this area [in Iceland] is where the Eurasian and North American tectonic plates meet, because I looked on this map. I'm guessing that there's been significant movement of those plates, and this volcanic eruption is the result."

Students deserve, at some point in every lesson, to experience the curriculum from the experts' perspective. This provides them with an opportunity to imitate the expert thinking.

Without the teacher's exposure of his thinking, his students would be left to their own devices to draw conclusions about the natural disaster they were witnessing. In a matter of two minutes, the teacher demonstrated how he used his background knowledge ("I'm thinking about how unique this eruption is"), consulted resources (the U.S. Geological Survey and a tectonic plate map), applied expert noticing ("See how it's tearing here?"), and speculated ("I'm guessing that there's been significant movement"). This teacher's use of a think-aloud procedure is a quality indicator of how expertise is shared in the classroom. Students deserve, at some point in every lesson, to experience the curriculum from the experts' perspective. This provides them with an opportunity to imitate the expert thinking, almost like an apprentice would in learning a new skill. Imitating is one of the ways humans learn, and modeling taps into this system (Fisher, Frey, & Lapp, 2008). Tips for effective think-alouds can be found in Figure 2.3.

Teachers regularly use modeling and demonstration to show students how a skill, strategy, or concept is used. While often associated more closely with performance tasks like swinging a tennis racket or playing a musical instrument, modeling is equally effective for cognitive and metacognitive tasks. Modeling includes naming the task or strategy, explaining when it is used, and applying analogies to link to new learning. The teacher then demonstrates the task or strategy, alerts learners about errors to avoid, and shows them how it is

Figure 2.3   Tips for Effective Think-Alouds

Choose a short piece of text. Think-alouds are often the most effective when they are focused and well paced. A brief think-aloud delivered using a passage of one to four paragraphs will have more impact because student interest will be maintained. As well, it will prevent the temptation to model too many strategies.

Let the text tell you what to do. Don't plan to go into a think-aloud cold, without having read the text, because your teaching points will be unfocused. Read the text several times and make notes about the comprehension strategies you are using to understand the text. These notes will provide you with ideas for the content of your think-aloud. Annotate the text so you will have something to refer to as you read.

Keep your think-alouds authentic. It can be a little disconcerting to say aloud what's going on in your head. Most teachers adopt a conversational tone that mirrors the informal language people use when they are thinking. An overly academic tone will sound contrived. It's better to say, "Hey—when I read this part about the penguins, right away I saw a penguin in my mind," rather than, "I was metacognitively aware and activated my visualizing strategy to formulate an image of a penguin as I read that paragraph."

Think like a scientist, mathematician, historian, artist, literary critic . . . Your shared reading texts are chosen because they have content value. Thinking aloud doesn't mean that everyone suddenly has to be a reading or English teacher. Make your think-alouds authentic by telling students how you process text through the lens of **your** content expertise. This elevates the think-aloud because you are showing them how your understanding of content text is influenced by what you know about the content.

Tell them what you did. Using an authentic voice doesn't mean you can't name the strategy. Tell your students what strategy you used to help you comprehend. This allows them to begin to form schemas about reading comprehension. Underline or highlight words or phrases that helped you understand and encourage students to do likewise, if possible.

Resist the urge to "over-think." The meaning of the passage should not be sacrificed for the sake of the think-aloud. Don't insert so many think-alouds into the reading that the intended message is lost. Fewer well-crafted think-alouds will have far more impact than a stream-of-consciousness rap that leaves the students bewildered by what just happened.

Source: Adapted from Fisher and Frey (2012b). ©2012. Reprinted by permission of Pearson Education, Inc., New York, New York.

applied to check for accuracy. Modeling is often accompanied by a think-aloud procedure (Davey, 1983) to further expose the decisions made by an expert as he or she processes information. For this reason, the think-aloud consistently contains "I" statements to invite the learner into the mind of the teacher.

This is a profound shift from what most teachers are accustomed to doing. Much of classroom instruction is in the second person and is interrogative in nature ("When you look at this eruption, what do you see?"). Teaching and quizzing become the order of the day, and students walk away from the class under the false assumption that somehow the teacher just "knows" the answer. They are not made privy to the speculative, at times hesitant, thinking of the content expert. What's lost are the natural stutter-steps made by someone who is deeply knowledgeable of the complexities of the topic.

It's understandable that many teachers struggle with this part of their instruction. The majority of instruction they have encountered has been the interrogative kind. They don't have an internalized monologue of what an effective think-aloud sounds like. Therefore, it's useful to introduce teachers to some quality indicators related to modeling and thinking aloud. We've found it particularly helpful for teachers to watch each other model and then talk about how it felt, both as the person modeling and the person observing expert thinking. Some of the indicators we look for during teacher modeling include

We've found it particularly helpful for teachers to watch each other model and then talk about how it felt, both as the person modeling and the person observing expert thinking.

- naming a strategy, skill, or task;
- stating the purpose of the strategy, skill, or task;
- using "I" statements;
- demonstrating how the strategy, skill or task is used;
- alerting learners about errors to avoid; and
- assessing the usefulness of the strategy or skill.

Importantly, after receiving adequate time in scaffolded instructional support that includes modeling, the students should be able to complete tasks using the skill or strategy that was modeled for them. In other words, modeling provides students with examples, not a recipe, that they can follow as they complete their own work.

Model Through Interactive Shared Readings

Shared reading is an instructional procedure that uses appropriately complex text that can be viewed by both the teacher and the student at the same time (Holdaway, 1979). The responsibility for reading the text is shared because the students follow the print silently while the teacher reads aloud. During subsequent rereadings, students can read aloud as well.

For younger students in kindergarten through second grade, an over-sized version of a picture book measuring approximately 24 inches or more in width is commonly used. The primary advantage of using a big book is that the large print and illustrations are visible to the students. Teachers of older students often display the shared reading text on a document camera, or many provide each child with a copy to write on. In other cases, a reading from the basal or a textbook is used. At all times, the passage chosen should be one that is complex in regard to its structure, its levels of meaning or purpose, its use of language conventions, or its high knowledge demand.

The interactive nature of shared readings allows teachers to move beyond simply conveying text to elevating a lesson to focus on discourse. Students at all grade levels benefit immeasurably from discussion with peers. These lessons are not passive, and they provide students with many opportunities to develop their academic language through the use of verbal expressions of ideas. In addition, they require students to listen closely not only to the text being read but to the comments of their peers as well.

Video 2.4

Making Learning Visible through Learning Intentions.
resources.corwin.com/ rigorousreadingtx

Characteristics of Interactive Shared Reading Lessons

Shared reading is recognizable in the way it is delivered by the teacher. A shared reading event is likely to be short and lively, and the text is read more than once to reinforce the skills or strategies being taught. It also helps students build the habit of rereading when the text is complex. As students become comfortable, they are encouraged to read along with the teacher. Rog (2001) describes five characteristics of shared reading:

- Uses large print
- Provides brief, engaging lessons that encourage student participation
- Suits mixed-ability groups
- Includes repeated readings to reinforce concepts
- Emphasizes skills at the letter, word, sentence, and text levels

A well-constructed interactive shared reading lesson serves as an effective method for introducing key strategies and skills through active teaching. Shared reading allows the teacher to instruct through modeling by demonstrating how a skill or strategy is applied to a reading. After modeling, the teacher asks questions to foster discussion and provides prompts to scaffold students' understanding as they read text that is initially new to them. Students interact with one another as well to support each other as they apply the new skill or strategy.

The act of shared reading does not create readers— it is what the teacher does inside the shared reading event that makes the difference.

Of course, it is essential to remember that the act of shared reading does not create readers—it is what the teacher does inside the shared reading event that makes the difference. Like all aspects of teaching, a successful shared reading lesson requires careful planning. Effective teachers

1. craft their lessons based on the needs of the students;
2. identify instructional materials that allow students to master the learning intentions; and
3. create a sequence of instruction that includes

   - modeling through demonstration,
   - scaffolding through questions and prompts, and
   - supporting through peer interactions.

In this way, students acquire important skills and strategies needed for accurate, efficient, and meaningful reading.

Pressley et al. (1992) observed a second-grade teacher use a think-aloud process during a shared reading of *Where the Wild Things Are* (Sendak, 1963). This text is complex in that it requires students to move back and forth between a realistic setting and a dreamlike one. The teacher used both visualization and prediction strategies to focus her students' attention on her anticipation of this shift:

> That night Max wore this wolf suit and made mischief of one kind and another . . . Boy, I can really visualize Max. He's in this monster suit and he is chasing after his dog with a fork in his hand. I think he is really starting to act crazy. I wonder what made Max act like that . . . Hm-m-m . . . I bet he was getting a little bored and wanted to go on an adventure. I think that is my prediction.

In a fifth-grade classroom, Ms. Fleck thought aloud during a shared reading to make her understanding of the opening paragraph of *Old Yeller*

(Gibson, 1956) explicit for students. Her modeling was designed to invite students into the book. The first paragraph of the book reads,

> We called him Old Yeller. The name had a sort of double meaning. One part meant that his short hair was dingy yellow, a color we called "yeller" in those days. The other meant that when he opened his head, the sound he let out came closer to being a yell than a bark. (p. 1)

We can model all we want, and do it well, but some students will still miss the point if they don't clearly understand the purpose of the lesson.

Ms. Fleck's think-aloud demonstrated the way in which a reader activates his or her prior knowledge, summarizes information, and predicts future events in the text. She said to the class,

> I like the way the author tells us how this dog was named— he got his name from the color of his fur *and* because of the sounds he makes. I think that is a great way to pick a name for a dog. I bet both of those things—his color and his bark—will be important as we read the story. The author is probably telling us this to get us ready for really important things in the pages to come. I had a dog like that. He used to make the most awful sound when he tried to bark. We never thought to call him "yeller," but wow, what a sound he could make.

Thus far we have discussed the reasons for modeling and the methods for doing so. But modeling requires active participation from the learner as well. We can model all we want, and do it well, but some students will still miss the point if they don't clearly understand the purpose of the lesson. A learning intention alerts the learner to what they should be attending to during your modeling, and how they will use it in their own learning. In the next section, we will examine the role of establishing learning intentions in order to ensure access to complex texts.

▶ Accessing Complex Text Requires a Clear Learning Intention

Each lesson should have a purpose, goal, learning intention or objective. We teachers have known about the importance of objectives for several decades (Hunter, 1976). A clearly articulated learning intention focuses instruction, provides students with an answer to the question "why do we have to learn this?" and allows for assessment of outcomes. It is a vital component for accessing complex texts, because it alerts students to what they should attend to as you model. In addition, it prepares them for the ways they will use the modeled information later in the lesson. Yet communicating the learning intention is a teaching behavior that is often neglected. In too many classrooms, students are left to intuit the learning intention of a lesson. Simply said, establishing the purpose of the lesson facilitates student achievement (Fisher, Frey, & Hattie, 2016).

Communicating the learning intention is a teaching behavior that is often neglected. In too many classrooms, students are left to intuit the learning intention of a lesson.

But what do good learning intentions look like? It's more than simply stating the standard to students. A quality learning intention statement provides information for students about what they will learn and how they might demonstrate that understanding. A quality learning intention statement also helps the teacher plan the lesson, as the tasks students are asked to complete should align with the expected understanding. This is an important point that is easy to overlook. The learning intention drives instruction, differentiation, and assessment. It might seem like an insignificant component of quality teaching, given that it should occupy only a fraction of the lesson, but we think it's the foundation of quality lesson planning and instructional delivery.

In our work, we use *learning intention*, rather than *goal* or *objective*, because it forces us to pay attention to what the students think. Teachers write objectives, but students have to know what the intent of the lesson is. While teachers want objectives that are measurable, students want to know what they're expected to learn and why. We ask our students, "What are you learning?" rather than "What are you doing?" because we want them to notice their learning. That's why an agenda or lesson plan alone won't do. It is a list of tasks, but it doesn't address the learning expectations or intentions.

Components of the Learning Intention

There are a number of ways to think about components of a learning intention. To be clear, the learning intention should not focus on the tasks that students will complete as part of the class session or at home. Rather, they should reflect the understandings that students will gain as a result of their engagement in the lesson components. When lessons are planned with the end in mind, learning intention are easier to develop (Wiggins & McTighe, 2005).

Content

Part of the learning intention comes from the content standards. This is, in part, why a clearly established learning intention is critical. Planning an amazing lesson for ninth graders based on seventh-grade standards will not ensure that the students reach high levels of achievement. Having a learning intention based on content standards ensures that instruction is aligned with high expectations.

Suggesting that the learning intention is based on the content standards does not mean that the learning intention *is* the standard. Most content standards take time to master. The learning intention should focus on the learning for the day. For example, it takes weeks for students to understand the causes and impact of World War II, so several learning intentions that add up to this larger picture will be required. When standards are not analyzed for their component parts and instead are used as the learning intention, students stop paying attention to them. The standards might be posted on the wall, but they're like wallpaper to students: a decoration that really doesn't have anything to do with today's work. An appropriate content learning intention for seventh graders might be to "Ask a question for clarification of facts and details after listening to a peer presentation." This is an important part of students' eventual understanding of Strand 1 (A), which reads, "listen actively to interpret a message and ask clarifying questions that build on others' ideas," but is not the whole standard, which will take much longer to accomplish.

Having a learning intention based on content standards ensures that instruction is aligned with high expectations.

Language

A second component of the learning intention relates to the ways in which students can demonstrate their understanding of the content. This is often referred to as the *language purpose*, as humans demonstrate their understanding by reading, writing, speaking, listening, and viewing. Understanding the linguistic demands of the content is critical for this component of the learning intention, which is especially valuable for English learners who are doing double the work, learning content and language simultaneously (Fisher, Frey, & Rothenberg, 2008).

To develop the language component of the learning intention, teachers should consider the following:

- Vocabulary
- Language structure
- Language function

For some lessons, the important linguistic component might be related to the *vocabulary* of the discipline. For example, in second grade, part of the learning intention might be for students to *use the terms time, place or location, or action when describing the setting.*

For other lessons, students need to focus on *language structure*—grammar, syntax, or signal words. For example, students learning the art of sourcing ideas might use a sentence frame, *While _____ believed _____, others disagreed* as part of their conversations with peers.

A third way to think about the language component is by determining the *function of language* that is necessary to understand the content. In other words, do students need to justify, persuade, inform, entertain, debate, or hypothesize to understand the lesson? For example, in a discussion about a particular text, part of the purpose might be to *justify your answer with evidence from the text.*

Social

The final aspect of the learning intention is the social purpose. Given that much of the learning students do will involve others and the fact that students need to learn prosocial behaviors, we believe that teachers should be clear about the expected social interactions students should have with their peers. There is a wide range of topics that students can learn socially, from taking turns to tracking the speaker to sharing ideas with others. The Texas speaking and listening standards provide some guidance for teachers in the selection of the social aspect of the learning intention. In addition, the social and emotional development of students should be considered as teachers plan lessons that include social learning expectations.

Sample content, language, and social purposes that comprise the learning intentions can be found in Figure 2.4.

The Texas speaking and listening standards provide some guidance for teachers in the selection of the social aspect of the learning intention.

Figure 2.4 Sample Content, Language, and Social Learning Intentions

	Content	Language	Social
Kindergarten	Notice where words start and stop	Use the *word space* or *punctuation* to identify the place where a word ends	Take turns when reading words in the sentences
Grade 5	Synthesize information from an informational text	Use sequence words (first, then, then, finally)	Track the speaker as he or she orally synthesizes information
English 2	Identify evidence from the text in support of your thesis	Justify the appropriateness of each piece of evidence	Provide growth-producing feedback to peers about their choices

Communicate the Learning Intention

Once a learning intention has been constructed, it has to be communicated to students. There are a number of ways that teachers do this. Some post it on the board and briefly talk about the learning intention and its relevance for students at the start of the learning intention. Others begin with inquiry and then invite students to talk about why they are doing what they're doing before making the learning intention more explicit. And still others verbally discuss the learning intention and then invite students to write the learning intention in their own words as part of their note-taking tasks.

Regardless of how the learning intention is established, it's important that students know the learning intention of the lesson. It tells them what to pay attention to and what will be expected of them as they learn to access complex texts. A clearly communicated learning intention increases the relevance of the lesson for students and helps the teacher remain focused on the lesson at hand without drifting too far afield and wasting valuable instructional time. In fact, this is the most common thing that teachers who begin communicating learning intentions tell us, "It really helped me stay focused." When asked about the impact of staying focused, we regularly hear "my students learn more" and "I have more than enough time to cover the standards, and cover them well." During the course of the lesson, unanticipated student misunderstandings may be revealed, and may necessitate deviation from the original instructional plan. However, even in these cases the learning intention is valuable, as it helps the teacher and the students return once again to the intended focus of the lesson.

A clearly communicated learning intention increases the relevance of the lesson for students and helps the teacher remain focused on the lesson without wasting valuable instructional time.

▶ Summary

The first access point for students to engage with complex texts is established through modeling and setting the expectations for learning. Modeling and thinking aloud provide students with a glimpse of your cognitive and metacognitive processes as you read, understand, and interact with a text. They also alert students to the fact that as an expert reader, you know you have to activate additional resources in order to make sense of the text. For that reason, it is helpful to identify in advance the elements of a text that you believe will give your students more difficulty. After all, they really don't need you to model what they already know how to do. Make sure that students witness how you solve comprehension problems and annotate the text to support subsequent readings. These efforts are likely to be wasted if students don't know what they are watching and listening for, or if they are unclear on how they will apply it. Clear learning intentions that address the content, language, and social demands of the lesson also assist students in focusing their attention.

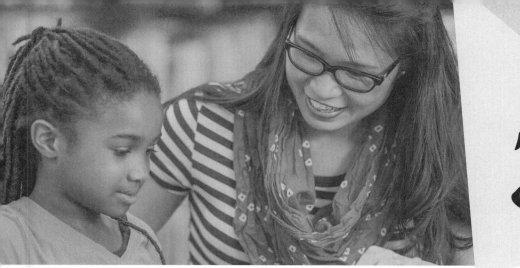

Access Point Two

Close and Scaffolded Reading Instruction

Middle school English teacher Armando Perez invites his students to read a short story called "Eleven" by Sandra Cisneros (1991). He points out to them that they are still exploring the inner lives of characters and considering how those lives compare to their outward lives—the ones that others can see. The students read the text independently, making notes as they go. Fernando underlines several sections in the text and circles two. Following their independent reading, Mr. Perez reads the text aloud to students, pausing to think aloud in the three places that seemed to have caused them confusion. He is able to pinpoint these particular sections of the text because he walked around the classroom observing his students as they made their annotations. He could thus target his modeling on these areas of confusion.

At one point, he pauses his read-aloud and says,

> They have a lot of years and numbers in this text, but
> this says that the sweater is maybe 1,000 years old. I'm

having a hard time believing that. I'm thinking that if it really were 1,000 years old, it would be in a museum. I'm thinking that this is an example of hyperbole that is being used to make a point.

Following his modeling, Mr. Perez asks his students to talk about a couple of questions, including "How is age like an onion, at least according to the author?" and "Why does she start crying when she has to wear the sweater?" The students talk with each other about these questions, often referring back to the text to locate specific information that they want to use in their responses.

Next, Mr. Perez asks students to talk with their team about Rachel's inner life, saying, "From what the author tells us, what can we surmise is going on inside Rachel's head when her teacher says that the sweater has to belong to someone?" The students focus on the words that the character Rachel uses to describe herself, such as "skinny," and on how the author refers to her "little voice." Jeremy says, "I don't think that Rachel has confidence because she stumbles on her answer to the teacher, and then it says that she's feeling like she is three again."

Close reading is predicated on the notion that the text is well known to the teacher and deeply understood. This can be challenging for teachers of younger students, who might be tempted to view these passages rather simply.

Mr. Perez continues inviting students to provide their arguments, with evidence, as they reread the text looking for examples. They talk with their groups often and periodically are invited to share with the whole class. After having read the text at least four times, Mr. Perez asks his students to use their annotations to describe the inner life of one of the characters in the short story. He says, "You might select Rachel, but alternatively you could select Mrs. Price or Sylvia or even Phyllis. Just remember to describe the character's inner life using evidence provided from the text." As the students get to work, Mr. Perez meets with several who have struggled with tasks like this in the past, making sure that they are starting on the right track.

There are many different ways to engage students in reading. There are instructional routines that require extensive teacher support, such as shared readings, which was described in the previous chapter, and instructional routines that require extensive peer support, such as reciprocal teaching or literature circles, which are included in the next chapter. In this chapter, we focus on an instructional routine called *close reading*, known in some circles as *analytic reading*. In addition, we will focus on scaffolded reading instruction.

Figure 3.1 Comparing Close and Scaffolded Reading Instruction

	Close Reading Instruction	Scaffolded Reading Instruction
Grouping	Large or small group; heterogeneous	Small, needs-based; homogeneous
Text Difficulty	Challenging, complex grade-level texts	Challenging but tailored to the instructional needs of the group
Teacher Supports	Text-dependent questions; annotation; repeated readings	Questions to check for understanding, prompts for cognitive or metacognitive work, cues to shift attention, and direct explanations as needed
Purpose	Expose students to content that stretches their thinking and reading skills	Advance student reading skill levels; practice comprehension strategies; uncover and address errors and misconceptions

This occurs in small groups. Both are useful in providing students access to complex texts. A comparison between close and scaffolded instruction can be found in Figure 3.1.

▶ Accessing Complex Text Requires Close Reading

Close reading is not a new instructional routine; in fact, it has existed for many decades as the practice of reading a text for a level of detail not typically sought after in everyday reading (Richards, 1929). Close readings should be done with texts that are worthy and that are complex enough to warrant repeated reading and detailed investigation. As Newkirk (2010) noted, not all texts demand this level of attention. But some texts do.

In those cases, the reader has to develop a fairly sophisticated understanding of what the author actually said. A problem, as described by advocates for close reading, is that students are often encouraged to answer questions that take them away from the reading prematurely and lead them to thinking about their own experiences. Instead, as Rosenblatt (1938/1995) recommended, there must be a transaction between the reader and the text. Readers should develop an understanding of the author's words and bring their own experiences, beliefs, and ideas to bear on the text. In her words, "The reader must remain faithful to the author's text and must be alert to the potential clues concerning character and motive" (p. 11). Rosenblatt cautioned that readers might ignore elements in a text and fail to realize that they are "imputing to the author views unjustified by the text" (p. 11).

If students already knew how to do this, we would not be spending time focused on close reading. The problem is that students do not arrive already knowing how to interrogate a text and dig down into its deeper meaning. Teachers have to teach students how to do this, in both informational and literary texts. In other words, close readings are not exclusively for English teachers; close readings should be conducted in any class or content area in which complex texts play a role, whether in science, social studies, auto mechanics, art, or physical education. Whatever the content may be, close readings of that content will always require the teacher to keep several important considerations in mind: the length of the selected text, the amount of time allocated for students to reread the text, the need to limit the frontloading of information when introducing the text, and the goal of having students annotate the text, ask text-dependent questions, and engage in text-dependent after-reading activities.

In the following section, we will describe six close reading practices that guide students' understanding of complex texts:

1. Short, worthy passages
2. Students rereading
3. Limited frontloading
4. Text-dependent questions
5. Annotation
6. After-reading tasks

Short, Worthy Passages

Because close readings can be time consuming, it is best to select shorter pieces of text for instruction. These selections, typically between three and nine paragraphs in length, allow students to practice the analytic skills required of sophisticated readers. Longer, extended texts can be used to encourage students to practice the skills that they have been taught during close readings. Close reading instruction is not limited to stand-alone

Video 3.1

Close reading with sixth-grade English language learners.
resources.corwin.com/ rigorousreadingtx

short texts such as news articles, poems, or short stories. Close readings can be done with short passages from longer texts, especially when a section is especially challenging and is pivotal for understanding the larger message of the text. Of course, this requires that the teacher analyze the text for its complexity and determine which parts require close reading. Close reading is predicated on the notion that the text is well known to the teacher and deeply understood. This can be challenging for teachers of younger students, who might be tempted to view these passages rather simply and not mine them for their more complex elements.

Students do not arrive already knowing how to interrogate a text and dig down into its deeper meaning. Teachers have to teach students how to do this.

Students' Rereading

As part of a close reading, students must read and reread the selected text several times. This requires that students have expanding purposes for each repeated reading. These rereadings can be completed independently, with peers, with teacher think-alouds, or any combination thereof. As noted in the example from Mr. Perez's classroom, complex texts do not give up their meaning easily or quickly. In addition to improving fluency, repeated readings contribute to the comprehension and retention of information (Millis & King, 2001) as well as enjoyment (Faust & Glenzer, 2000). The practice of rereading carries into adult life, as noted by Smith (2000), who found that to be one of the most common strategies adults use to understand text. Of course, there are a number of ways to facilitate students' rereading of the same text. Unfortunately, most readers do not like to reread things a second or third time unless there is a specific reason for doing so. During close readings, the purpose for each reading is made clear, and often, those purposes are related to looking for evidence in response to a specific question. Importantly, rereading also reduces the need for extensive frontloading.

Limited Frontloading

When students read a piece of text only one time, the teacher has to do a lot of work to ensure their understanding. In other words, the teacher is doing the heavy lifting. When students read and reread a text multiple times and talk about the text with their peers, the teacher does not have to provide as much instructional support. The rereading, discussions, and text-dependent questions do some of this. During close readings, the teacher does not provide much in the way of pre-teaching or frontloading of content. The structure of the lesson itself is the scaffolding that was once delivered through frontloading.

As with inquiry, the goal of close reading is for students themselves to figure out what is confusing and to identify resources they can use to address their confusions. It is essential that they develop the meta-cognition needed to understand difficult texts. Close reading is in part about discovering—in this case, discovering what the author meant and how to come to terms with the ideas in the text. For example, students were introduced to George Washington's "Farewell Address" in their humanities class. Consistent with a close reading approach, students read and discussed this text several times, over several days, to fully develop their understanding of the text and what role it played, and continues to play, in history. Had their teacher provided a great deal of information in advance of this reading, students might have skipped the reading entirely and focused on what the teacher said.

Revealing the content of the reading in advance is different from stating the *learning intention*. Learning intentions focus on the reasons for reading but do not provide the students with all the information about the reading. In the first lesson, the learning intention was for students to identify Washington's reasons for leaving office after his first term as president. However, he withheld the details of the content of the passage itself. In addition, had the teacher told students what to think about the text (a common problem with extensive pre-teaching), the investigative aspect would have been lost, and students would not have developed the thinking skills that they needed when encountering complex texts on their own. Through multiple readings, students were eventually able to identify the influential nature of the document on the Federalist Party development.

Close reading does not apply solely to informational texts. Consider the difference in the amount of student learning that would likely occur in following two scenarios: first, in a situation where students are told about the author's life, his reason for writing, and the historical significance of a sonnet such as "The Long Love" by Sir Thomas Wyatt; second, in a case where students are given a chance to encounter the text and struggle with the meaning. In the former, students are often told what to think, whereas in the latter, students are guided in their discovery. In an eleventh-grade British literature class, as this poem was discussed, one student said to another,

Video 3.2

Students rereading and discussing a complex text in high school English.
resources.corwin.com/ rigorousreadingtx

Video 3.3

Close reading of historical information.
resources.corwin.com/ rigorousreadingtx

The lines in this poem that stand out to me are "And in mine heart doth keep his residence," and "And therein campeth, spreading his banner." These lines stand out to me because they both are examples of how Wyatt uses love as a person, not just a feeling. Using the word "his" to refer to love as someone that is within him. It's like he's possessed with love.

Later in their discussion, the students were asked to consider the extended metaphors in the poem. They had experience analyzing the metaphors in the text, understood what they were being tasked with, and were able to apply this knowledge to the poem. Another student responded,

> The major metaphor of the poem, I feel, is consistent because Wyatt talks about love as a thing living within him, within his heart and throughout the poem that does not change. At the end he even says, "But in the field with him to live or die?" Wyatt refers to love as his master and will follow him into the field.

The archaic language of the poem made this more complex, and it would have been tempting to teach students about the meaning of the poem in advance of their readings. But by allowing students to wrestle with, and ultimately discover, that the poet was writing about the all-consuming power of romantic love to turn a life upside down, these students were able to locate the poem's meaning for themselves. Grounded in the text, they are now ready to extend their thinking about connections to themes in literature and in their own experiences. Too much frontloading, in this case, might have prevented this learning. However, the students didn't come to these understandings simply through rereadings and through their teacher's practice of limited frontloading. Their teacher relied on text-dependent questions to provide students with expanding purposes for rereading, and to guide their thinking.

The goal of close reading is for students themselves to figure out what is confusing and to identify resources they can use to address their confusions. It is essential that they develop the metacognition needed to understand difficult texts.

Text-Dependent Questions

As part of every close reading, students should discuss their responses to text-dependent questions that require them to provide evidence from

Video 3.4

Close reading and text-dependent questions in upper elementary school.

resources.corwin.com/ rigorousreadingtx

Accessing complex texts doesn't mean simply having them nearby—readers actually have to read them.

the text rather than solely from their own experiences. For example, if a British literature teacher asked students the personal question, "Have you ever been in love?" he would have derailed the class discussion before it even began. Most of us can imagine the chaos that would have ensued as a roomful of 17-year-olds gleefully chomped down on this question. However, a commitment to fully understanding the text will still lead students to find answers to these sorts of questions as they begin to see themselves and the world within the words of another (you couldn't prevent them from making these connections even if you tried!).

The types of questions students are asked influence how they read a text. If students are asked only recall and recitation questions, they learn to read for that type of information. If they are asked questions that require them to analyze, synthesize, and evaluate, they learn to read more closely and actively engage with the text. Unfortunately, many of the questions that students are asked are about personal connections, which may not even require them to have read the text at all. We are interested in questions that require students to locate evidence within the text. These text-dependent questions require a careful reading of the text such that students can produce evidence in their verbal or written responses. This is not to say that personal connections should be avoided at all costs. After all, readers naturally compare the information they are reading with their experiences. However, the argument for text-dependent questions asserts that discussions (and writing prompts) should focus on the text itself to build a strong foundation of knowledge. This purposefully built foundational knowledge can then be leveraged by learners to formulate opinions and make connections that are meaningful and informed.

As an example, consider the following two questions a teacher *could* ask of her students who have been studying an essay from *Last Call at the Oasis* (Weber, 2012) titled "A Way Forward? The Soft Path for Water" by Peter Gleick:

- Has your family made any changes to reduce water consumption?
- What are the differences between soft and hard paths to water management?

The first question can be answered without ever reading the essay. A conversation about the first question may be very animated and interesting, but it does not require that the students develop any level of understanding of the information presented by the author. If you were to observe this lesson, you might witness significant student engagement in a class discussion about the first question. But consider whether the actual text factored into the discussion or remained sitting on their desks unused. Accessing complex texts doesn't mean simply having them nearby— readers actually have to read them. Asking questions that require students to have to read and understood the text is crucial. The first question about family water consumption habits is actually irrelevant within the context of this essay, which focuses on systemic water conservation methods. It is important that as teachers we know how to engage students, beyond simply asking them to tell a personal story. The content itself can and should be used to engage.

The emphasis should be on getting students to use explicit and implicit information from the text to support their reasoning.

There are several ways to structure questions such that students return to the text to find evidence for their responses. We caution that these questions should not focus solely on recall. The emphasis should be on getting students to use explicit and implicit information from the text to support their reasoning. There are at least six categories of text-dependent questions that can be drawn from and structured into a progression that will move students from understanding explicit meaning to understanding implicit meaning, and from working at the sentence level to working across an entire text and even with multiple texts. As well, some of these question types may not be suitable for a particular reading; there is no requirement that all of these types need to be used with every piece of text. Figure 3.2 contains a graphic of these questions. Further, as students discuss a given text, they will likely cover many of the questions that could have been asked. When they do so, the teacher does not need to ask a prepared question. We like to think of the prepared text-dependent questions as a resource that the teacher has to scaffold students' understanding and hope that much of the classroom conversation addresses the content of the question. The question samples below are based on the water essay referenced above. Examples of text-dependent questions for texts at the elementary grade levels can be found in Figure 3.3.

As noted in Figure 3.2, there are three overarching questions that we use to organize the flow of a close reading lesson. The lesson starts at the literal level, with the first two question types (general understanding and key details). Students should be thinking, "What does the text say?" When

Figure 3.2 Text-Dependent Questions

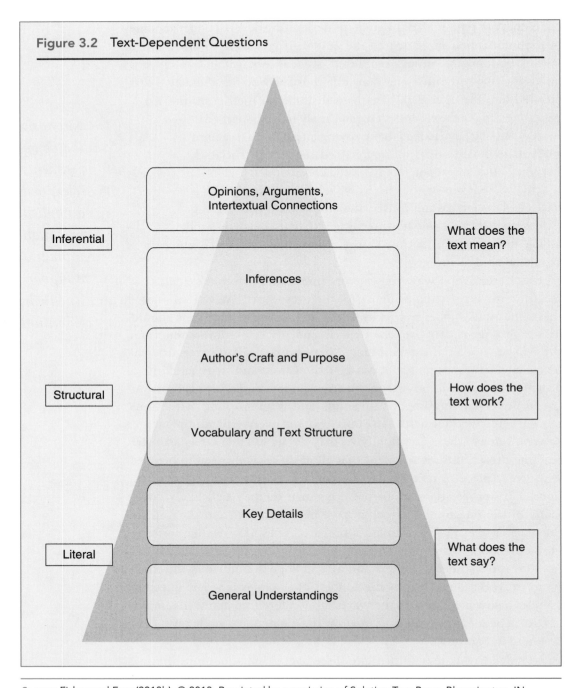

Source: Fisher and Frey (2013b). © 2013. Reprinted by permission of Solution Tree Press, Bloomington, IN.

Figure 3.3 Sample Text-Dependent Questions

Question Type	Questions From *Frog and Toad Together* (Lobel, 1971) in First Grade	Questions From Chapter 10 in *A Night to Remember* (Lord, 1955) in Sixth Grade
General Understandings	Retell the story using *first, next, then*, and *finally*.	Why would the author title the chapter "Go Away"?
Key Details	What ways did they try to solve the problem of eating too many cookies?	What are two things that could have prevented this tragedy?
Vocabulary and Text Structure	How did the author help us to understand what *willpower* means?	How does the chronological structure help the reader understand the events?
Author's Craft and Purpose	Who tells the story?	Whose story is most represented and whose story is underrepresented?
Inferences	Do you think Toad's actions caused the seeds to grow? Why?	Why would Mrs. Brown run lifeboat number 6 with a revolver?
Opinions, Arguments, Intertextual Connections	In your opinion, is Frog a good friend to Toad? Do you think this is a happy story or a sad one?	Compare this book with *Inside the Titanic* (Brewster & Marschall, 1997). What are the similarities and differences?

Source: Fisher and Frey (2012a). © 2012. Reprinted by permission of the International Literacy Association, Newark, Delaware.

the teacher has evidence that students have mastered the literal level of the text, the questions should shift to the structural level. Sometimes the teacher will have evidence from students' annotations that they understand the text at the literal level and thus should move on. Other times, the first literal question provides sufficient evidence of students' thinking. And still other times, the teacher will need to ask several literal questions to scaffold students' understanding of the text. Teachers should always have more literal questions ready than they probably need, because it's hard to predict when students will get stuck, and having questions ready prevents teachers from telling students what to think about the text.

Teachers should always have more literal questions ready than they probably need, because it's hard to predict when students will get stuck.

Following the literal level, the discussion and analysis moves to the structural level with the over-arching question of "How does the text work?" In this phase, the focus is on vocabulary, text structures, author's craft, and author's purpose. These are the choices that authors make as they construct a text. As readers explore the answers to these questions, the text becomes a mentor, and student writing will likely improve.

The final phase of the close reading focuses on the inferential level of understanding. This is where teachers want to get their students. But starting at this level can frustrate students and result in teachers telling students what to think. If the text is sufficiently complex, it won't give up its meaning easily, and the journey from literal to structural to inferential will scaffold students' understanding so that the teacher can guide the experience rather than directly explain the reading to students.

In the section that follows, we'll explore each of the question types that make up the three phases of a close reading lesson.

General Understandings

These questions get at the gist of the text. What does the author want us to know or understand from the text? Often, these questions focus on the main claim and the evidence used to support the claim or the arc of the story or the sequence of information. For the water essay, the teacher might ask,

"Which is the water path recommended by Gleick?"

Interestingly, this question is not directly addressed in the essay, and students will have to find clues from across the text to figure out his main claim. Alternatively, the teacher might direct students in this way:

"Discuss the ages of water and why Gleick believes we are headed into the third age."

As implied in the structure of this directive, text-dependent work does not need to take place solely in a whole-class setting. Students can be encouraged to discuss their thinking with their peers. This particular exercise will lead students to a more clear-cut answer, but the act of engaging in the discussion is central to getting them to understand the essay and the key point that the author is trying to make.

Key Details

These questions focus on asking students about the important details that the author uses to inform the reader. Often these questions include who, what, where, when, why, or how in the stem. They can also include reference to the more nuanced details that must be understood to add clarity to the reading. For example, the following question is key to understanding Gleick's perspective:

"What is the difference between water and water services?"

The teacher might also ask this:

"What is one method Gleick identifies for reducing water consumption?"

Key detail questions tend to focus on information presented directly in the text. Importantly, understanding this information should be critical to understanding the text; key detail questions should not focus simply on trivia. As well, these key details should be used to scaffold students' understanding as they respond to more complex questions.

Vocabulary and Text Structure

Some of the questions that students must consider revolve around the vocabulary used by the author, as well as the structure of the text itself. Text structure questions require that students consider the organization of the reading, such as the use of problem/solution or character dialogue to propel action. In asking questions related to vocabulary, teachers must be sure to make reference to both denotations (definitions)

If the text is sufficiently complex, it won't give up its meaning easily, and the journey from literal to structural to inferential will scaffold students' understanding so that the teacher can guide the experience.

and connotations (the ideas or feelings that a word invokes) of words. In addition, as appropriate, the questions may focus on shades of meaning, word choice, figurative language, idioms, and confusing words or phrases. Finally, questions can provide students an opportunity to use context or structural clues to determine the meaning of unknown words. For example, the teacher might ask students about the three key ideas discussed in the essay about water:

> "After reading this essay, how would you summarize the differences between productivity, efficiency, and supply?"

Alternatively, the teacher might ask students to determine the meaning of the word *ozonation* from the context clues or to discuss why the author chose the word emerged when talking about *Homo sapiens* over time. In addition, the teacher might ask students to comment on the structure of the essay and to note the differences between the parts in terms of tone and structure. Attentive students would notice those sections of the text with significant descriptions, with a reliance on problem/solution structures, and with a persuasive tone.

Author's Craft and Purpose

Inference questions require that students have read the entire selection so that they know where the text is going and how they can reconsider key points in the text as contributing elements of the whole.

The genre of the text and the use of narration help students make sense of what they are reading. So does the analysis of point of view and literary devices. On the flip side, understanding the overall purpose of the text guides students in following the flow of the reading. Readers should understand if the text is meant to inform, entertain, persuade, or explain something to them. There are also situations in which the text has a specific bias or provides only part of the story. In these situations, students could be asked about the perspectives not explored in the text. For the water essay, some examples of questions related to the author's purpose are as follows:

> "How does Gleick attempt to convince readers that water is a worthy issue of discussion?"

> "What is Gleick's purpose in writing this? Is he trying to inform, entertain, or persuade? How do you know?"

> "Is Gleick biased? What is your evidence?"

> "Does Gleick acknowledge other perspectives? If so, what is the effect? If not, how does that influence your reaction to the piece?"

Inferences

Some of the questions that students need to think about require that they understand how the parts of a text build to a whole. Unlike the cognitive processes associated with inference at the local level, these inferences require students to consider the piece as a whole. They probe each argument in persuasive text, each idea in informational text, or each key detail in literary text, and anchor them to the central themes of the piece. Importantly, inference questions require that students have read the entire selection so that they know where the text is going and how they can reconsider key points in the text as contributing elements of the whole. In the Gleick essay, students might be asked questions like these:

> "How does the information at the start of the essay, about the U.S. using less water today compared with 30 years ago, help Gleick make his argument for the third age of water?"

> "How does Gleick use the six differences between hard and soft paths to build the case for water services?"

Opinions, Arguments, and Intertextual Connections

The final category of text-dependent questions should be used sparingly, and typically comes after students have read, and reread, a text several times to fully develop their understanding. Readers should have opinions about what they read, and they should be able to argue their perspective using evidence from the text and other texts, experiences, and beliefs that they hold. For example, while reading about water, the teacher might ask questions like these:

> "Did Gleick make a convincing argument about the ages of water?"

> "Is there sufficient evidence presented that a soft path is the appropriate direction?"

> "How do Gleick's recommendations compare with those presented in the essay 'In Our Lifetime: Deconstructing the Global Water Crisis and Securing Safe Water for All' by Gary White?" (Weber, 2012)

These questions should result in deep and engaging conversations, especially when students have read and understood the text. Over time and with practice, students will begin asking themselves and their peers these types of questions, and the teacher will not be the only one who poses questions for discussion.

Annotation

In the last chapter, we recommended modeling annotation as a way to teach students how to interact with the text and how to interrupt the passive reading experience that can leave many of them struggling to find the meaning of a complex piece of text. Readers with a passive stance expect that the information will wash over them, and when it does not, they throw in the towel. Marking up the text allows them to witness their own growing understanding, and it encourages them to put into words what they do not yet understand. Annotation occurs first during their first or second pass at the text, but should also continue throughout subsequent discussion framed by text-dependent questions.

Readers with a passive stance expect that the information will wash over them.

For example, in an eighth-grade unit of study on adolescence, humanities teacher Paula Brown used several pieces of text that allowed her students to practice their annotation skills. She had previously modeled annotation with several other pieces of text, print and digital, and felt they were ready to begin using it themselves. As she told her students,

Adolescence is a time when important decisions—some of them life changing—occur. It can be scary to think that some of the choices you make now can last a lifetime. In this unit of investigation, you will explore what a parent, a poet, and a psychologist have to say about making decisions that seem small at the time, but are big in hindsight. The purpose of this unit is to examine adolescent decision-making from three perspectives in order to locate central themes.

As part of this unit, students read and annotated an article titled "Psychologist Explains Teens' Risky Decision-Making Behavior" (Iowa State University, 2007). For example, a section of Javier's text was annotated in this way:

Gerrard said that the initial risk-taking experience will influence an adolescent's intention to repeat the behavior in the future. They do consult their conscience over risk-taking, but not always in a classic "good vs. evil" way.

"From a kid's perspective, if you're operating in this more reasoned, thoughtful [experienced] mode—then you have the proverbial devil and the angel over your shoulder," she said. "If you're operating in the more experiential [impulsive] mode, you don't even know the angel is there. Those things are not in your mind at all, and the devil's only saying, 'This could be interesting.'" *EX*

After their first couple of readings through the text, Ms. Brown engaged students in a discussion using text-dependent questions, which encourage them to reread, and to consult their annotations, to deeply comprehend the passage. As part of their discussion, Ms. Brown asked students to consider the following questions, requiring that they provide evidence from the text for their responses:

- **General Understandings:** *What is the main finding of Dr. Gerrard's research?*
- **Key Details:** *What role does image play?*
- **Vocabulary and Text Structure:** *How did you figure out what* impulsive *and* reasoned *mean?*
- **Author's Craft and Purpose:** *Why is this genre appropriate for the content? Who is the intended audience for this article?*
- **Inferences:** *How can you determine that this is a credible source?*
- **Opinions, Arguments, and Intertextual Connections:** *Let's compare this article to the first reading we did ("Who's Right?"). How does this informational article explain some of the conflict occurring between mother and daughter?*

Marking up the text allows students to witness their own growing understanding, and it encourages them to put into words what they do not yet understand.

Throughout the discussion, the teacher reminded her students to mark up their text because "we read with our eyes, our brains, our hearts, and our pencils." She stated that the action of annotation gives them a sense of ownership and influence over the text and lowers the sense of intimidation that some readers feel when confronted with a difficult reading: "I want you to know that a reading shouldn't ever boss you around. I want you to see evidence of your growing understanding of the text as we get further into the discussion."

After-Reading Tasks

Rather than take students away from the text, post-reading activities should require them to return to the text. For example, students may write an argumentative piece in which they use evidence from the text. They may engage in a Socratic Seminar or debate a topic. After-reading tasks should help students consolidate the meaning of texts and deepen their comprehension far beyond what they would be able to accomplish on their own.

Having students create short written summaries of complex texts provides them with an opportunity to solidify their understanding and to develop a catalog of notes for comparing multiple pieces of text in the future. You will recall that Paula Brown's unit on adolescence included three pieces of text. She noted, "It's hard for them to make comparisons across documents when they don't have meaningful notes, so I often have them do some précis writing so they'll have useful writing to draw from later in the unit." Following their discussion on the article written by the psychologist, Ms. Brown asked her eighth-grade students to summarize their understanding of the text. She told her students, "Write a short summary of about 100 words that accurately summarizes the article. Be sure to include the name of the researcher and the findings. And remember to use your annotations to guide your writing."

As literacy educators, you have to ensure that students are engaged in reading texts that are worthy of their time.

Précis writings are summaries of a text or passage that require students to distill the main points but also involve them in the process of "selecting, rejecting, and paraphrasing ideas" (Bromley, 1985, p. 407). Teaching students how to compose précis writings develops their ability to understand the text more deeply and to learn essential content. These writing tasks do not contain the student's opinions or questions and should not include any information not discussed in the text itself. The students in Ms. Brown's class will later use these précis writings to produce a longer essay in which they address the topic of adolescent decision making from different perspectives.

Close readings are an important component of reading instruction, but they are not the only instructional routine that students need to experience to become successful readers. As literacy educators, you have to ensure that students are engaged in reading texts that are worthy of their time. You also have to ensure that students investigate the text sufficiently to really develop an appropriate level of understanding. Combined with shared, collaborative, and independent readings, close readings provide students the experiences they need to become skilled in analytic reading, a prerequisite for college and career success.

Close Reading for Young Readers

Thus far, the examples we have offered have involved older students, but if you are a primary teacher, you may be thinking, "How could this ever occur with my students?" K–3 students have an especially wide gap between the level of texts they can read on their own and those they can read with some adult support. In other words, they can understand narrative and informational texts that far outstrip their current reading levels. In most cases, the teacher is the reader of the text during a close reading lesson for students in the primary grades. Much of the literacy instruction during the primary grades focuses on foundational language skills, especially through scaffolded small-group, needs-based reading instruction as well as whole-class lessons on "word structure knowledge through phonological awareness, print concepts, phonics, and morphology." But close reading does something else for students in the primary grades: it develops their listening comprehension and thinking skills. At that age, students' listening comprehension far exceeds their reading comprehension. The close reading lessons allow students practice with comprehension skills (strand 2) while also practicing their listening, questioning, and sharing (strand 1). One example is the use of *The Wonderful Wizard of Oz* (Baum, 1900/2000) in kindergarten. No one would expect five-year-olds to read this book on their own, or even with adult support. Rather, the intention is to expose young students to complex texts that challenge their thinking skills rather than their reading skills. Perhaps we should refer to this as *close listening*, because so much of this is about listening comprehension.

Read-alouds such as this should not be confused with the soothing after-lunch read-alouds teachers sometimes use. Being read aloud to plays an important role in reading for pleasure, and most of us have fond memories even decades later of read-aloud experiences such as this. We do not advocate that this practice be abandoned. However, we do advocate the addition of read-alouds that are designed to develop the critical thinking skills these students will use across their reading lives. We are referring to interactive read-alouds (Fisher, Flood, Lapp, & Frey, 2004) that require students to actively participate in the co-construction of knowledge and understanding in ways that are similar to the close readings described in

The intention is to expose young students to complex texts that challenge their thinking skills rather than their reading skills. Perhaps we should refer to this as close listening, because so much of this is about listening comprehension.

the section above. Close listening (reading) lessons use an interactive think-aloud approach that draws from many of the same principles as those used for older students:

Video 3.5

Close reading in the primary grades.

resources.corwin.com/ rigorousreadingtx

- Uses short, worthy readings that are complex due to structure, use of language conventions, levels of meaning, or knowledge demand
- Requires the text to be reread several times throughout the lesson
- Frames discussion and deepens student understanding of the text through the use of text-dependent questions
- Relies on after-listening tasks that require students to draw on knowledge of the text

Figure 3.4 provides a comparison between close reading in the primary grades and lessons that are developed for older students.

Kindergarten teacher Mohamed Hassan uses readings from Aesop's fables to promote close listening. "These short tales are great for my kids during the first few months of school," he said. "They challenge them to really listen closely to get the details." He cited "The Lion and the Mouse" as an example.

"The version I use has some tough vocabulary in it, like *gnawed*, and *plight*, and *bound*," he said. "Great general academic words." He continued, "So I give them an introduction, really just a reminder about what we already know about how these fables work, so we're always looking for the moral of the story." The story is less than 200 words long, and after reading it to them twice, he fosters a discussion using text-based questions:

- **General Understandings:** *What happened? Tell me the story using your own words.*
- **Key Details:** *How did the lion help the mouse? How did the mouse help the lion?*
- **Vocabulary and Text Structure:** *What does the mouse mean when he says, "Perhaps I might be able to do you a turn one of these days?"* (Mr. Hassan said that he rereads the story again to them after posing this question.)
- **Author's Craft and Purpose:** *What is the moral of the story that Aesop wants us to know?*
- **Inferences:** *Why is the lion so surprised at the idea that a mouse could help him? What does the lion say and do that helps you answer this question?*

Figure 3.4 Comparing Close Reading in Primary and Upper Grades

Close Reading in Primary Grades	Elements	Close Reading in Upper Grades
The reading level of the text is significantly higher than students' reading level.	**Text Selection**	The text complexity is slightly higher than what the student takes on during other phases of reading instruction.
The teacher is reading the text aloud to students, although they are not grasping its deeper meaning. The text may or may not be displayed.	**Initial Reading**	Students are more likely to read the text independently, although they are not fully grasping its deeper meaning.
The teacher guides annotation practices using displayed text and fosters collaboratively developed annotations.	**Annotation**	Students familiar with annotation practices are marking the text independently and adding to their annotations throughout class discussions.
The teacher reads the text aloud multiple times. Students may read along at the paragraph, sentence, phrase, or individual word level. A few students may read the text independently in subsequent readings due to practice effects.	**Repeated Readings**	Students are rereading independently or with minimal support. Students may also have access to audio supports (a poet reading her poem, a teacher reading dialogue, a peer reading a key sentence).
Text-Based Discussions		
Students engage in extended discussion, which is driven by text-dependent questions and dialogic teaching. Students deepen their understanding through analysis of the literal, structural, and inferential dimensions of the text.		
Students draw and write collaboratively and independently, with adult support and guidance. They engage in shared investigations and debate compelling questions.	**Responding to Texts**	Students write collaboratively and independently. They investigate and research and debate compelling questions.

Mr. Hassan uses students' knowledge of the traditional telling of this tale, with its more difficult language structures, to introduce them to a wordless illustrated version of the story. "Sometimes I use an animation video with the sound turned off, and other times there is a print version available. Depends on the story," he added. In this case, he used Pinkney's (2009) *The Lion and the Mouse*. "Now they are retelling the story with each other using the illustrations, and it's amazing to hear them use more sophisticated language in their oral retellings because they know the original version so well," he said. "That use of oral language skills is so important in getting their reading off the ground."

Students are developing their reading skills, and they need experiences with texts that are still complex but may not be as far up the proverbial staircase of complexity as the texts that are used in close reading.

While annotation isn't featured when using read-alouds, it can be a part of a shared reading experience that gives students visual exposure to the text. Poems on chart paper, projected readings, and texts that come in the form of big books all have a role in close reading in primary grade classrooms. Interactive SMART Boards have annotation features that are easily used by students, and low-tech items such as highlighting tape and reusable wax sticks work well in temporarily annotating large print items.

The first half of this chapter has been dedicated to close reading practices that guide students' understanding of complex texts. A key feature of this type of instruction is the use of text-dependent questions that draw students back into the reading. It's really the progression of the questions themselves that guides student thinking. But students are also developing their reading skills, and they need experiences with texts that are still complex but may not be as far up the proverbial staircase of complexity as the texts that are used in close reading. This needs-based practice, called *scaffolded reading instruction*, relies on questions, prompts, and cues to foster students' cognitive and metacognitive skills.

▶ Accessing Complex Text Requires Scaffolded Reading Instruction

In scaffolded reading instruction, small groups of students with similar learning needs are grouped together for a short time to receive specific instruction from the teacher using text that will require instruction and support. These materials may include leveled texts for students in the primary grades (K–2) and complex texts, textbooks, or other readings the teacher has gathered for students in grades 3 and beyond. The purpose of scaffolded reading instruction is to deliver customized lessons based on recent assessment information. These assessments may be collected during the scaffolded reading instruction lesson itself or at other times during the day.

The major work of young readers is in melding foundational skills and comprehension skills to understand text. Consolidation of these skills is essential for emergent and early readers to master, and at times challenges with foundational skills, such as decoding, can impede their ability to fully access the text. Small-group scaffolded reading instruction is an ideal time to accomplish both.

First-grade teacher Alma Fernández uses small-group homogenous grouping to provide scaffolded reading instruction for four students she has gathered for customized phonics instruction that is tied to a text she will be using for shared reading. Based on her most recent assessment results, these students require additional attention. Her class will be reading *A Bike Like Sergio's* (Boelts, 2016) about a boy who faces a moral dilemma about whether to return money he found to the rightful owner or keep it for himself to purchase a bike. The text has complex concepts in it and will be a great story for prompting meaningful discussion. She previewed the first five pages of the text for her whole class yesterday afternoon, thinking aloud about the problem Ruben, the main character, will soon face. They are eager to dig into it today. However, Ms. Fernández knows that these students are having difficulty with initial and final consonant blends and digraphs. "They won't be reading the book entirely independently, but I don't want them to be tripped up with some of the phonics demands," she explains.

Ms. Fernández identified several such words featured in the book: *breath, wish, bread, blue, shuffle, float,* and *floor*. She has written these words on flashcards, and each child has a small magnetic whiteboard in front of them, in addition to blank index cards. She has also duplicated the first five pages of the story so that each child has a copy. The teacher introduces the words and tells the children that these words appear in the text they'll be reading together. For the next 15 minutes, Ms. Fernández moves her students through several phonics activities as they manipulate the words: constructing them with magnetic letters, isolating the blends and digraphs using the blank index cards as sliding doors to frame letters, fast-paced flashcard games, and writing some of the words themselves. Now, using the text, the children use colorful highlighters to mark the words they have been practicing. Finally, Ms. Fernández rereads the first five pages to them, pausing as she encounters a targeted word for them to supply. "This is a preview for them in advance of our reading this afternoon," she explains. "I'm always conscious of how important it is to tie decoding to comprehension," she continues, "so they can access the text meaningfully."

Scaffolded reading instruction typically lasts between 10 and 20 minutes, depending on the needs and stamina of the students. Stamina is a legitimate consideration for scaffolded reading instruction because this intensive instructional time may be the most cognitively demanding time of the day for students. In secondary classrooms, where instructional periods are far shorter than the 120 minutes allocated in elementary classrooms for reading instruction, a teacher may meet with only one group each period. However, these meetings are not limited to students who struggle with reading. In fact, all students benefit from this responsive instructional arrangement that allows the teacher to provide scaffolds with precision when needed and to withhold them when they are not necessary.

Scaffolded reading instruction can be used in secondary classes to guide collaborative reading groups. The students in Mike Sawyer's seventh-grade English class are organized in literature circles to read and discuss books related to the unit theme of Taking Responsibility. One group has selected *Stargirl* (Spinelli, 2003). Mr. Sawyer's observation of their last group meeting prompted him to meet with the five student members for additional scaffolded reading instruction. "They were stuck on condemning the students in the story who shunned Stargirl, but they weren't getting to a major understanding I had hoped would emerge by this point in the novel," he said. "They weren't really seeing that Stargirl's unorthodox character represented a part of what the others wished they could be but weren't brave enough to do."

Mr. Sawyer met with the group and asked them to reread the opening pages silently. "Sometimes there are these huge ideas that are represented at the very beginning, but we pass right over them because we don't know the story yet. As you read, can you find a line or two that is more meaningful to you now that you're nearly done with the book?" After a few minutes, Kendra offers, "Well, I'm not sure, but there's this line on page 2. 'It did not occur to me that I was being watched. We were all being watched.'" The teacher asks, "Why do you believe that's an overlooked gem?" and Kendra and the group engage in a conversation about self-consciousness and being observed. "I guess we get hung up on being worried more about what other people think," offers Jake.

"Now I'm going to ask you to make a big shift in the book, to chapter 9," says the teacher. "There's this extended passage about frogs that live in the mud in the desert," he continues. "Spinelli describes them as *dormant.*

How does the line in chapter 1 link to the discussion about frogs? I mean, who cares about frogs? But we know authors rarely put in details that have no usefulness." The group is silent at first, but then Troy ventures, "Maybe it's like everyone is hiding in the mud?" Kendra finishes his thought. "Like they're not really alive because they're too self-conscious?" His students have made an important conceptual shift as they begin to understand more fully why the shunning has occurred. "So they're not bad people, like evil," says Troy. "But they're afraid, and not really awake to who they really are," adds Antonio. The teacher smiles, as he senses that the next literature circle discussion will be enriched because of the time he spent with them in scaffolded instruction. "Sometimes it's just the catalyst they need to make these big leaps in understanding," said Mr. Sawyer.

In the following section, we will describe in more detail the principles and practices that guide effective scaffolded reading instruction:

- The student, not the teacher, is the reader.
- Small groups help differentiate support.
- Students have similar strengths and needs.
- Grouping patterns change frequently.
- Using questions and providing prompts and cues guide learners.

We will also discuss why *whole-class* scaffolding reading instruction creates difficulties.

The Student, Not the Teacher, Is the Reader

Everything in a scaffolded reading instruction lesson is designed to lead to the student reading the text. Often, this is accomplished through silent reading. The teacher may designate stop points in the text so the group can discuss the reading and clarify misunderstandings. Not surprisingly, this is not realistic with emergent readers who do not read silently, or with early readers who are just beginning to do so. Therefore, it can be tempting to have each student take a turn and publicly read a portion of the text. This practice, called *round robin reading*, is an ineffective and potentially detrimental approach to reading instruction (Optiz & Rasinski, 2008).

Another practice, called *choral reading*, refers to the practice of having students read in unison. Choral reading can be an effective tool for building

It can be tempting to have each student take a turn and publicly read a portion of the text. This practice, called round robin reading, is an ineffective and potentially detrimental approach to reading instruction.

fluency through repeated readings, especially in reader's theater. It is also an appropriate strategy for dramatic performances such as the recitation of a poem. Its usefulness is limited in scaffolded reading instruction, however, because the purpose here is to provide more individualized support for students. There may be brief passages that lend themselves to choral reading, particularly alliterative sentences or rhyming passages that beg to be heard aloud. That said, the student-reading portion of the scaffolded reading instruction lesson should be devoted to the individual.

Small Groups Help Differentiate Support

The purpose of holding scaffolded reading instruction groups to no more than six is to ensure that the teacher can provide more direct contact time with each learner. When group sizes grow beyond this number, management demands may take precedence over instruction. In addition, the small size of the group allows the teacher to observe each student up close in the act of learning. Insight into a learner's problem-solving skills can inform future instruction because the teacher gains an understanding of what the students do when they get to a "tricky part."

Although the group should not exceed six, it is acceptable for it to be as small as one student. This is especially true when working with students who significantly struggle with reading. While it may be tempting to place all the lowest-achieving students in one group, it is likely that they require more individualized instruction than their grade-level peers because their skill profiles are more idiosyncratic. In our experience, normally progressing readers tend to have a great deal in common with one another, whereas those who struggle tend to be unique in their patterns of strength and areas of need.

As we will discuss in the next chapter, the students who are not with the teacher in scaffolded reading instruction can be collaborating with their peers or working independently. Scaffolded reading instruction should not result in hours of independent work for the rest of the class.

Students Have Similar Strengths and Needs

Most commonly, teachers form scaffolded reading instruction groups based on similar literacy strengths and needs, called a *homogeneous group*. This is done for two reasons: practicality and peer support. It is practical because the teaching day simply does not have enough minutes in it to allow for individual instruction for each student. Small-group structures also capitalize on the power of peer influence on learning. Stated another

Video 3.6

Teacher working with groups of students to facilitate their understanding.
resources.corwin.com/ rigorousreadingtx

way, students benefit from the questions and insights of their peers in a teacher-directed group.

Grouping Patterns Change Frequently

We have stated that students are grouped based on a number of considerations, especially student strengths and needs. It is also vital to remember that these grouping patterns should not be static. In other words, the scaffolded reading instruction group a child belongs to in September should not be composed of the same classmates in May. It is essential for students to benefit from numerous opportunities to learn with one another; flexible grouping patterns ensure this happens. It is equally critical that students see themselves as contributors to the learning of others; flexible grouping patterns ensure this happens as well. Of course, careful consideration about how students are grouped is only a small part of scaffolded reading instruction. These groups are formed to implement powerful forms of teaching in which questions, prompts, and cues are used to provide students access to complex texts.

Using Questions and Providing Prompts and Cues Guide Learners

Students need experiences with a range of complex texts—not just the ones highlighted for close reading, which are quite complex. During scaffolded reading instruction, teachers provide more support and guidance than they do during close reading. This requires a teacher who can listen carefully to what students are saying to give them just enough support to let them find the answer. At the heart of scaffolded reading instruction lies the strategic use of questions to check for understanding, prompts to trigger cognitive and metacognitive thinking, and cues as needed to shift attention more overtly (Fisher & Frey, 2010b). In other words, rather than relying on text-dependent questions and repeated reading for the scaffolds—as is the case in close reading—the teacher provides support by attending to the misconceptions and errors that students make. Scaffolded reading instruction also provides students with practice applying comprehension strategies while learning to resolve their confusions.

Video 3.7

Teacher using prompts and cues to guide learning.

resources.corwin.com/ rigorousreadingtx

Questions to Check for Understanding

The subject of questioning is critical to scaffolded reading instruction because questioning is the very core of the instruction. Once students have finished the reading for the lesson, teachers should pose literal and inferential questions to them. Retelling is a query at the *literal* level and is closely associated with comprehension. Teachers should invite students to retell and encourage them to use their books to support their retelling. Readers should return to the text as needed, and this should be considered an acceptable classroom practice. For instance, asking how the Big Bad Wolf disguised himself in *Little Red Riding Hood* is an example of a literal question.

In addition, ask questions that require students to *infer* meaning about the text, such as questions that ask about the main idea, or about the author's purpose for writing the book. An example of an inferential question for the same book is inquiring about why the wolf chose to disguise himself as an old woman and not a young man. Questioning may also probe students' reactions and opinions of the text. Asking a reader about his or her thoughts concerning talking to strangers encourages students to form an opinion and to provide evidence for their responses. Although every question you may ask cannot be anticipated in advance, it is useful to prepare literal and inferential questions to begin meaningful discussion with students.

Scaffolded reading instruction begins when the teacher poses a question to check for understanding. This is not the time to assess students but rather a time to uncover misconceptions or errors. Students should be asked a variety of questions to check their understanding, and teachers should be continually on the lookout for misconceptions and errors.

For example, when Meghan Becovic asked a group of students to explain how they knew if something was living, she wanted to uncover their understanding of the scientific definition of life, a concept they had been reading about. When her students provided her with a number of correct responses, she changed direction asking, "So is evolution a characteristic of life?" When several students nodded positively, she knew that she had uncovered a misconception that she needed to address. There are a number of question types useful in checking for understanding, such as *clarifying* and *elaboration* questions in which students are encouraged to add details and examples to their answers. When students are asked to clarify or elaborate on their responses, misconceptions, errors, and partial understandings will reveal themselves.

Prompts for Cognitive or Metacognitive Work

When errors or misconceptions are identified, the first step in resolving them is to prompt the student to engage in mental work, either cognitive or metacognitive. Unfortunately, in too many classrooms, when errors

---

It is useful to prepare literal and inferential questions to begin meaningful discussion with students.

Video 3.8

Having Successful Collaborative Conversations.
resources.corwin.com/ rigorousreadingtx

Video 3.9

Teacher working with small groups of students to generate questions.
resources.corwin.com/ rigorousreadingtx

are identified, teachers skip the prompts and cues and instead provide the missing information for students. In this case, the student has not done any of the work and likely did not learn anything from the exchange. Teachers can prompt students' background knowledge and experiences, the rules they have been taught, or the procedures commonly used to solve problems (Figure 3.5 contains a list of common prompts used during scaffolded reading instruction). For example, when Frank Acerno questioned his students about a science article they were reading, he uncovered a misconception about speed versus velocity. In prompting them, he asked, "Remember the animation we watched about driving to school? Velocity and speed have some things in common, but . . ." The students immediately responded with a quote from the animation, "velocity is speed with direction," and their misconception was resolved.

When students are asked to clarify or elaborate on their responses, misconceptions, errors, and partial understandings will reveal themselves.

Cues to Shift Attention

If prompts fail to resolve the error or misconception, teachers can assume a more directive role through the use of cues. Cues should shift students' attention to something they've missed or overlooked (Figure 3.6 contains a list of common cues used during scaffolded reading instruction). A simple cue might be, "Take a look at the figure on page 112. Does that help?" There are a number of cues that are effective, including gestural, verbal, visual, physical, environmental, and positional. Of course, teachers use these cues regularly in their initial teaching, but often fail to use them when students are stuck. While reading an article on migration during the U.S. westward expansion, Terri Goetz identified an error that was not resolved through prompting. She used her voice and a gesture to shift students' attention. While pointing to a graph, she said, "Population PER thousand," emphasizing the word *per* with her voice.

Direct Explanations

Sometimes, prompts and cues do not resolve the errors or misconceptions that students have. In those cases, students cannot be left hanging. Teachers must ensure that students have a successful learning experience, even if that means providing a direct explanation and giving the student the answer. Importantly, direct explanations should come after prompts and cues to increase the likelihood that students can connect this new information to a thinking process in which they were engaged.

Figure 3.5   Types of Prompts

Type of Prompt	Definition/When to Use	Examples
Background knowledge	Used when there is content that the student already knows, has been taught, or has experienced but has temporarily forgotten or is using incorrectly.	• As part of a science passage about the water cycle, the teacher asks, "What do you remember about states of matter?" • When reading about a trip to the zoo, the teacher asks, "Remember when we had a field trip to the zoo last month? Do you recall how we felt when it started to rain?"
Process or procedure	Used when established or generally agreed-on rules or guidelines are not being followed and a reminder will help resolve the error or misconception.	• The student is saying a word incorrectly, and the teacher says, "When two vowels go walking. . . ." • When the student has difficulty starting to develop a writing outline, the teacher says, "I'm thinking about the mnemonic we've used for organizing an explanatory article."
Reflective	Used to encourage students to be metacognitive and to think about their thinking, which can then be used to determine next steps or the solution to a problem.	• The student has just read something incorrectly, and the teacher asks, "Does that make sense? Really think about it." • When the student fails to include evidence in her writing, the teacher asks, "What are we learning today? What was our purpose?"
Heuristic	Used to help learners develop their own way to solve problems. These are informal problem-solving procedures. They do not have to be the same as others' heuristics, but they do need to work.	• When the student has difficulty explaining the relationships between characters in a text, the teacher says, "Maybe drawing a visual representation of the main character's connections to one another will help you." • When a student gets stuck and cannot think of what to write next, the teacher says, "Writers have a lot of different ways for getting unstuck. Some just write whatever comes to mind, others create a visual, others talk it out with a reader, and others take a break and walk around for a few minutes. Will any of those help you?"

Source: Adapted from Fisher and Frey (2013a). Used with permission of ASCD.

Figure 3.6 Types of Cues

Type of Cue	Definition	Example
Visual	A range of graphic hints that guide students through thinking or understanding.	• Highlighting places on a text where students have made errors • Creating a graphic organizer to arrange content visually • Asking students to take a second look at a graphic or visual from a textbook
Verbal	Variations in speech used to draw attention to something specific or verbal attention getters that focuses students thinking.	• "This is important . . ." • "This is the tricky part. Be careful and be sure to . . ." • Repeating a student's statement using a questioning intonation • Changing volume or speed of speech for emphasis
Gestural	Teacher's body movements or motions used to draw attention to something that has been missed.	• Pointing to the word wall when a student is searching for the right word or the spelling of a word • Making a hand motion that has been taught in advance such as one used to indicate the importance of summarizing or predicting while reading • Placing thumbs around a key idea in a text that the student was missing
Environmental	Using the surroundings, and things in the surroundings, to influence students' understanding.	• Keeping environmental print current so that students can use it as a reference • Using magnetic letters or other manipulatives to guide student's thinking • Moving an object or person so that the orientation changes and guides thinking

Source: Adapted from Fisher and Frey (2013a). Used with permission of ASCD.

Following the direct explanation, the teacher should monitor students' understanding by asking them to repeat the information back in their own words or asking the original checking for understanding question again. In this way, students are accountable for the information and for processing the experience with their teacher.

The Trouble With Whole-Class Scaffolded Reading Instruction

The process we outlined above works best with small groups of students. It's a difficult process to put into place in a whole-class setting. While checking for understanding can be done effectively with the whole class, when the teacher moves to prompt or cue, some students disengage. Some students don't need the information that their teacher is providing right now, either because it's not relevant or because they already understand the concept. When some students disengage, they distract others. Improving classroom management, however, won't improve this situation. Unless scaffolded reading instruction is done quickly and expertly and all of the students have a task to do while the teacher prompts and cues those who need it, some students will lose focus. It's just human nature. It's better to address misconceptions or errors with small groups of students or individually, especially while students work collaboratively or independently.

When the teacher moves to prompt or cue, some students disengage.

Returning to the life science teacher, Meghan Becovic, and the students' misunderstanding of the definition of living, prompts and cues were used to ensure their eventual understanding. At one point, Ms. Becovic asked her students to identify the characteristics all living things share. Part of their conversation follows:

Jamal:	One thing for life is breathing.
Teacher:	Do all things breathe? Think about that.
Mubarik:	Yes. We have to breathe or die.
Teacher:	So, I'm thinking about plankton.
Anais:	No, some things don't breathe.
Mubarik:	Oh, yeah, I forgot. But there is a word for what I'm thinking.
Jamal:	Is it metabolism?
Mubarik:	Yeah, that's it. To be alive you have to have metabolism.
Anais:	Yeah, that was in the book. I remember now.

Teacher:	Is metabolism the same as evolution?
Jamal:	No, but living things have to evolve or die.
Anais:	Wait a minute. We said that before, that they will die.
Teacher:	Take a look on this page [pointing to a website displayed on a computer].
Mubarik:	It says that living things have to reproduce. It doesn't say nothing about evolution.
Jamal:	So, maybe things don't have to evolve to be alive. Maybe that's more long term, not if the thing is alive right now.

As their conversation continued, the students in this group reached greater understanding of the content because their teacher did not simply tell them the missing information but rather scaffolded their understanding through prompts and cues. We have to be sure we provide this type of support for students who are stuck. When this is not provided, students become dependent on adults for information. When this support is provided, students become independent thinkers and learners who thrive inside and outside of the classroom.

▶ Summary

Close reading and scaffolded reading instruction establish critical access points to complex texts because they begin the shift of responsibility to the learner. Through the process of close reading, students are learning to stay close to the text to gain knowledge. These close reading lessons can be done in whole-group or small-group settings, and it is the text itself that is the predominant source of information. But students are also acquiring the skills of reading, and they need practice in drawing on their own cognitive and metacognitive resources as they read. This is achieved through scaffolded reading and requires the teacher to offer supports that encourage students to use what they already know as well as what the text has to offer.

Access Point Three

Collaborative Conversations

Four sixth-grade students are deeply involved in a discussion about the book they are reading in their literature circle, *The Music of Dolphins* (Hesse, 1996). The story centers on a young girl who has been raised in warm Caribbean waters by a school of dolphins. Named Mila by her rescuers, she is brought to a facility to be studied by scientists who are interested in the language development of feral children. However, Mila hopes to escape this bewildering environment and return to the only family she has ever known.

David opens the conversation. "In chapter 53, Mila begs Doctor Beck to let her go back to the ocean, but the doctor says she can't because she will go to prison. What did all of you think about that?"

"I think Mila said it best on page 163—'I look at her. I am already in prison.' Mila feels trapped, like she's suffocating," offers Estefany.

Marisol holds up her notebook for everyone to see.

That sentence meant a lot to me, too. I drew a picture of a girl in a cage at the zoo as I read that. I was remembering her conversation with her friend Justin, when he asked her if she got tired of people coming to look at her all the time.

David asks another question when the group gets quiet. "Reynaldo, do you have an idea to add?" At this, Reynaldo responds,

Well, I wrote this in my notebook: "Mila feels like she's just a thing, not a person, and that nobody except for Justin even tries to see her as anything more than a dolphin girl. It feels that way in school sometimes, when everyone is checking everyone else out and deciding whether they're cool or not. It's like no one even bothers to look past your clothes or hair or where you live."

These students are participating in a collaborative learning format called *literature circles* (Daniels, 2002). In between meetings, they read independently and make notes in their notebooks to be used in the next discussion. Each meeting is moderated entirely by the students themselves, who determine the direction of the conversation and the next reading task. In this way, students collaborate with one another to access complex texts.

Collaborative learning is one of the critical linchpins through which students access complex text because it enables them to consolidate their understanding with peers and provide support for one another in the absence of the teacher. We use the term collaborative learning in reference to work done with peers. These peer-assisted learning opportunities furnish students with a means of applying the skills and strategies they have learned during modeling, close reading, or scaffolded instruction. Collaborative conversations are a vital facet of group learning.

▶ Accessing Complex Texts Requires Collaborative Conversations

Increasing the amount of time students talk using academic language has been a priority for decades (see Fisher, Frey, & Rothenberg, 2008, for a review). Simply said, students need practice with academic language if they are to become proficient in that language. We don't only mean in English class; students must learn to speak the language of science, history,

Video 4.1

Teacher introduces literature circles.
resources.corwin.com/ rigorousreadingtx

mathematics, art, literature, and technical subjects if they are to become thinkers in those disciplines (Fang, 2012).

From the time that there have been educational standards, speaking and listening have been included. In other words, this is not new. What is new is the role that student-to-student interaction plays in the standards. Although there is a great deal of attention paid to the reading and writing standards, we believe that educators should also attend to the increased demands placed on the speaking and listening domain, especially in strand 1, which requires that students "work collaboratively with others" starting in kindergarten and continuing through English IV.

There is much to note in this standard, including the fact that most grades have specific expectations for the development of oral language. There are some cases, such as in grade 9 and 10 for area D, in which the standard is the same for two years. Some key points noted in these standards are:

Video 4.2

Teaching students to collaborate.
resources.corwin.com/rigorousreadingtx

- Students are expected to collaborate. This means that there needs to be instructional time devoted to student-to-student interactions.
- Students are to understand the rules of a discussion early in their development and then use those skills throughout their lives. The standards do not specify the rules of discussion, but tracking the speaker, taking turns, rephrasing ideas, asking clarifying questions, and so on are good skills for students to learn in this area.
- As students get older, they are expected to include evidence in their responses. This means that they have to develop ways to keep track of the evidence as they read. Annotations can help with this, as can note taking and other forms of discussion guides.
- There are a number of "soft skills" included in this standard that will also serve students well. For example, developing a plan for consensus building, planning agendas, and setting time limits for speakers will help ensure that the collaborative learning that students do will be productive.

Students need practice with academic language if they are to become proficient in that language.

The way this is operationalized in different grades is presented in Figure 4.1. We have bolded words and phrases that did not appear in the standards

Figure 4.1 Strand 1: Developing and Sustaining Foundational Language Skills: Listening, Speaking, Discussion, and Thinking—Oral Language

English IV Students:	**C. formulate sound arguments and present them using elements of classical speeches such as introduction, first and second transitions, body, conclusion, the art of persuasion, rhetorical devices, employing** eye contact, speaking rate such as pauses for effect, volume, enunciation, purposeful gestures, and conventions of language to communicate ideas effectively
	D. participate collaboratively, offering ideas or judgments that are purposeful in moving the team toward goals, asking relevant and insightful questions, tolerating a range of positions and ambiguity in decision making, and evaluating the work of the group based on agreed-upon criteria.
English III Students:	C. give a formal presentation that **exhibits a logical structure, smooth transitions, accurate evidence, well-chosen details, and rhetorical devices** and that employs eye contact, speaking rate such as pauses for effect, volume, enunciation, purposeful gestures, and conventions of language to communicate ideas effectively
	D. participate collaboratively, **offering ideas or judgments that are purposeful in moving the team toward goals, asking relevant and insightful questions, tolerating a range of positions and ambiguity in decision making, and evaluating the work of the group based on agreed-upon criteria.**
English II Students:	C. give a **formal** presentation **that incorporates a clear thesis and a logical progression of valid evidence from reliable sources and that employs** eye contact, speaking rate such as pauses for effect, volume, enunciation, purposeful gestures, and conventions of language to communicate ideas effectively
	D. participate collaboratively, building on the ideas of others, contributing relevant information, developing a plan for consensus building, and setting ground rules for decision making.
English I Students:	C. **give a presentation using informal, formal, and technical language effectively to meet the needs of audience, purpose, and occasion,** employing eye contact, speaking rate such as pauses for effect, volume, enunciation, **purposeful gestures,** and conventions of language to communicate ideas effectively
	D. participate collaboratively, **building on the ideas of others, contributing relevant information, developing a plan for consensus building, and setting ground rules for decision making**
Grade 8 Students:	C. **advocate a position using anecdotes, analogies, and/or illustrations** employing eye contact, speaking rate, volume, enunciation, a variety of natural gestures, and conventions of language to communicate ideas effectively
	D. participate collaboratively in discussions, **plan agendas with clear goals and deadlines, set time limits for speakers, take notes, and vote on key issues**

Grade 7 Students:	C. **present a critique of a literary work, film, or dramatic production**, employing eye contact, speaking rate, volume, enunciation, a variety of natural gestures, and conventions of language to communicate ideas effectively
	D. engage in meaningful discourse and provide and accept constructive feedback from others
Grade 6 Students:	C. give an organized presentation **with a specific stance and position**, employing eye contact, speaking rate, volume, enunciation, natural gestures, and conventions of language to communicate ideas effectively
	D. participate in student-led discussions by eliciting and considering suggestions from other group members, taking notes, and identifying points of agreement and disagreement
Grade 5 Students:	C. **give an organized presentation** employing eye contact, speaking rate, volume, enunciation, natural gestures, and conventions of language to communicate ideas effectively
	D. work collaboratively with others to develop a plan of shared responsibilities
Grade 4 Students:	C. **express an opinion supported by accurate information**, employing eye contact, speaking rate, volume, enunciation, and the conventions of language to communicate ideas effectively
	D. work collaboratively with others **to develop a plan of shared responsibilities**
Grade 3 Students:	C. **speak coherently about** the topic under discussion, **employing eye contact, speaking rate, volume, enunciation**, and the conventions of language to communicate ideas effectively
	D. work collaboratively with others by following agreed-upon rules, **norms, and protocols**
Grade 2 Students:	C. share information and ideas **that focus on** the topic under discussion, speaking clearly at an appropriate pace and using the conventions of language
	D. work collaboratively with others by following agreed-upon rules for discussion, including listening to others, speaking when recognized, making appropriate contributions, **and building on the ideas of others**
Grade 1 Students:	C. share information and ideas **about the topic under discussion**, speaking clearly **at an appropriate pace** and using the conventions of language
	D. work collaboratively with others by following agreed-upon rules for discussion, including listening to others, **speaking when recognized, and making appropriate contributions**
Kindergarten Students:	C. **share information and ideas by speaking audibly and clearly using the conventions of language**
	D. work collaboratively with others by following agreed-upon rules for discussion, including taking turns

Source: Texas Education Agency.

for the previous grade to highlight the instructional components for each grade. For example, students in grade 2 are expected to participate in "building on the ideas of others," which was not the expectation for students in grade 1 or kindergarten. Similarly, the grade 6 standard adds "with a specific stance and position" to the presentation skills that were developed in grade 5.

Other grades have major differences between them. For example, grade 6 students are expected to "give an organized presentation," whereas grade 7 students must "present a critique of a literary work, film, or dramatic production." To ensure that students develop mastery of the standards, teachers must understand the specific expectations for students by grade level. Analyzing the differences by grade level, known as vertical alignment, is critical if teachers are going to develop teaching points aligned with the standards. Some people have argued that the speaking and listening standards are less important than the reading and writing standards because the state tests reading and writing but not speaking and listening. This is a problematic stance, as Biemiller notes: "Oral comprehension sets the ceiling on reading comprehension." Britton said it another way: "Reading and writing float on a sea of talk." In other words, as students' listening comprehension improves, so does their potential for reading comprehension. That's why collaborative conversation is an access point to complex texts.

For collaborative learning to work, teachers must structure the time students have to interact with their peers to work toward these new skills. We will limit our conversation about collaborative learning to those structures and habits that provide students increased access to complex texts. There are a host of collaborative learning routines that provide this type of access, and some that are useful in other ways. That said, it is important to recognize that students must be taught to collaborate with their peers.

Building Structures for Collaborative Learning

"I'm just not sure they're really doing anything of value when they're in groups."

This is perhaps the most frequent reservation we hear from educators when the subject of student collaboration comes up. Worried about the amount of instructional time dedicated to a group project, some teachers question whether it is better to simply tell students what they need to

Video 4.3

Introducing partner talk.
resources.corwin.com/ rigorousreadingtx

know. But telling alone isn't especially effective. Other teachers possess a fixed idea about the task itself, believing incorrectly that for the work to be worthwhile, it must extend over several class periods. Still others express concerns about individual students who prefer to work alone rather than in a group. Armed with these misgivings, many teachers list the benefits of group work, and then offer an apology: "It just doesn't work for the students I teach."

These apprehensions prevent otherwise innovative educators from deepening their instructional practices. And many of these qualms are rooted in the potential issues surrounding task complexity. Some teachers worry about logistic and behavior problems if the task is too easy or too difficult. They question the value of the learning itself, wondering aloud whether it's worth the fuss. And, at times, they may even question whether their students are capable of sustained group work without the constant presence of an adult. Addressing *task* complexity is key to ensuring that the time devoted to productive group work is in fact productive (Frey, Fisher, & Everlove, 2009). Quality indicators of appropriate task complexity take the following factors into account:

We suggest that teachers post, teach, and revisit norms for interaction, especially those that explain how to debate and disagree without being disagreeable, and how to seek, offer, accept, and decline help graciously.

- Designs that require students to work together
- Structures that elevate academic language
- The presence of grade level work
- The opportunity for productive failure

Designs That Require Students to Work Together

Group tasks require the same sort of thoughtful design process that goes into other aspects of instruction. First and foremost, students need to know how to interact with one another and how to seek help. We have sometimes heard teachers remark that they shouldn't have to teach about the norms of interaction, as "students should know how to work with each other by now." This is true, but only to a point. While students may have ample experience with group work in previous grades, they don't yet know how to work *for you*. Therefore, we suggest that teachers post, teach, and revisit norms for interaction, especially those that explain how to debate and disagree without being disagreeable, and how to seek, offer, accept, and decline help graciously.

It is important that teachers keep task complexity in mind when introducing new routines to students. Students who are learning a new way to work with one another should not be challenged with demanding content at the same time. The task complexity itself should be temporarily lowered to make it possible for students to attend to the collaborative learning processes and procedures that are new to them.

Structures That Elevate Academic Language

Video 4.4

Teacher outlining expectations, especially for language usage.

resources.corwin.com/ rigorousreadingtx

Students also need to know how to use the academic language of the lesson. Students of any age or level of experience benefit from language scaffolds that encourage them to use academic language and vocabulary. The use of language frames (partially constructed statements and questions that frame original ideas) is highly effective during collaborative conversations. In particular, teachers may find that students need sentence starters as they get used to using argumentation in their discussions. These language frames can be posted on table tents or on chart paper. For example, Karen Jessop provided her students with the following frames when they wanted to offer a counter claim:

- I disagree with _____ because _____.
- The reason I believe _____ is _____.
- The facts that support my idea are _____.
- In my opinion _____.
- One difference between my idea and yours is _____.

Ensure Grade-Level Work

When students are engaged in productive group work, the expected level of rigor for a given task should be made clear. It really doesn't matter how good the instruction is if students in a fifth-grade class are working on third-grade-level content. The result is predictable—the students will have learned third-grade information, not fifth-grade information. Although we understand that there are students who currently perform below grade level, lowering expectations is not the way to close the achievement gap. Some students require scaffolded reading instruction, which involves the teacher using questions, prompts, cues, and direct explanations. As we noted in the previous chapter, students can be grouped based on assessed needs, and the teacher can focus on those needs with small groups. Other students require supplemental or intensive intervention, which is the focus of the Response to Intervention efforts under way in most districts (Fisher & Frey,

2010a). Importantly, while students are working productively with their peers and have peer support and language brokers, they should be working on tasks and texts that facilitate their understanding of grade-level concepts. The texts that are used in collaborative conversations and peer learning should be suitably complex for where the students are within the school year. Keep in mind that the collective work of the group is to make meaning together, and, accordingly, the texts used can and should be more complex than those texts students have used in their independent reading.

Consider a task Mr. Bonine's life science students completed as part of their unit on energy in an ecosystem. Each group of students was provided an envelope that contained little slips of paper with words on them. The words on the slips of paper were terms for different organisms in an ecosystem. Students were asked to sort the words in any categorical system that made sense to them. As group members moved words into categories, they had to defend their placement to their peers. They were encouraged to use a language frame, "This organism, _____, belongs in the _____ category because _____." When Imani moved the paper with the word bacteria to a new column, she said, "This organism, bacteria, belongs in a new category because it doesn't fit in any of these others." Her team members agreed, putting their thumbs up to show their agreement.

That's what collaborative learning should do: It should provide students with an opportunity to consolidate their understanding of rigorous concepts so that they can access increasingly complex texts.

Once students had their categories, Mr. Bonine introduced technical vocabulary, including the terms *autotroph* and *heterotroph*. He asked students to re-sort their organisms based on this new information. Spenser moved all of the words back to a pile, saying, "These categories of predator and prey don't work for this. This organism, zooplankton, belongs in the heterotroph category because it can't make organic compounds. Instead, it eats other organisms."

During the period, Mr. Bonine added additional terms, such as *decomposer* and *producer*, and asked his students to continue their sorts. In doing so, the students in this biology class completed tasks designed to ensure their learning of grade-level biology concepts. He then moved them into a complex reading on these concepts, a science piece on the use of heterotrophs for recycling and biodiesel production, and students met in small groups to discuss the article. And that's what collaborative learning should do: It should provide students with an opportunity to consolidate their understanding of rigorous concepts so that they can access increasingly complex texts.

Video 4.5

Students working collaboratively on a presentation.
resources.corwin.com/ rigorousreadingtx

Design for Productive Failure

"Failure" may seem antithetical to education, but we consider its presence a quality indicator of task complexity. In much the same way that we recognize that we often learn from our mistakes, so it is with the learners in our classrooms. The growing research on productive failure in learning is that students who initially fail at a task are more receptive to subsequent instruction, as evidenced by increased achievement and performance (Kapur, 2008). Importantly, we don't want students to experience this failure in isolation. The best time for them to do so is during collaborative learning.

Collaborative learning isn't just pushing desks together and then calling it a day. Collaborative learning hinges on the complexity of a given task and the degree to which students cognitively engage with it.

A task designed with the possibility of productive failure in mind must be one that is sufficiently novel. In other words, it should not be a mere reproduction of what the teacher just did. A problem with reproductive tasks is that they are susceptible to the "divide and conquer" or the parallel independent work approaches in which so many groups engage. In these scenarios, the task itself is already known; now it's just a matter of students following the steps—no thinking required. Groups with this mindset merely divide up the task, go their separate ways, and then get back together to assemble the final product.

For the task to possess the possibility of productive failure, it must also be designed to require interaction and teamwork. The text students are using should be complex enough that they actually need each other to broker an understanding of it. It is important to listen in on a group that is wrestling with a text that is difficult enough to possibly fail. In doing so, you'll likely hear students discussing the content, not just the task. They will use academic language and vocabulary in ways that indicate they are cognitively engaging with the topic. Ideally, they will also ask questions of one another, offer explanations and clarifications, and provide evidence to support their claims. To be sure, making this quality indicator a reality in your classroom requires getting close to groups to hear how they apply their knowledge to solve problems. But this is essential to more fully understanding the quality of learning that is occurring in your classroom.

Collaborative learning work isn't just pushing four desks together and then calling it a day. A truer measure of the value of collaborative learning hinges on the complexity of a given task and the degree to which students cognitively engage with it. The complexity of the task ensures they have something to talk about; the structure of the task provides them the forum for doing so.

Key Elements of Collaborative Learning

Although there is a strong research base on the effectiveness of peer-assisted learning that takes place in cooperative and collaborative groups, it is also widely recognized that it is challenging to implement the kinds of grouping scenarios that give rise to this learning. Like all good instruction, collaborative learning requires careful planning to ensure success for teachers and students. We have included a checklist in Figure 4.2 for you to use as you consider the key elements of the planning process. Below, we will discuss in more detail those related to grouping, goal setting, and the accountability measures.

Effective teachers tell us that when they are making grouping decisions, they consider how the group might receive help when faced with a difficult task.

Grouping

One of the first decisions a teacher must make when using collaborative learning has to do with how to pair or group students. Should the groups be composed of students working at a similar level (homogeneous grouping) or of differing levels (heterogeneous)? Effective teachers tell us that when they are making grouping decisions, they consider how the group might receive help when faced with a difficult task. In teacher-directed groups such as scaffolded reading instruction, that help is available in the form of the teacher because he or she is working with students at the time. However, in collaborative learning, the students are working apart from the teacher, and help is not as easily obtained. Therefore, the help must emerge from within the group. This help is more likely to occur in mixed-ability pairs or groups. This advantage of mixed-ability groups has been articulated in student feedback as well. In a study of grouping preferences of more than 500 elementary schoolchildren, Elbaum, Schumm, and Vaughn (1997) reported that students preferred mixed-ability groups (especially pairs) to homogeneous groups. On a related note, Bennett and Cass (1989) found that having specific ratios of students with particular ability levels was also important to heterogeneous groups. They noted that the optimal group was composed of two lower-performing students and one higher-performing student. In groups where the ratio was reversed (two higher-performing students to one lower-performing one), the lone struggling student was often left out of the activities. It is interesting to note that the higher-achieving students performed equally well in both circumstances.

Goal Setting

Successful collaborative learning pairs or groups understand what their goals are for the task at hand. Be sure to give groups specific directions

Video 4.6

Reciprocal Teaching: Predict and Question.
resources.corwin.com/ rigorousreadingtx

Figure 4.2 Planning Checklist for Collaborative Learning

❒ What text will students be using?

❒ What are my learning intentions for the group?

- Academic

- Social

❒ What is the task?

❒ Where do the groups fit into my instructional sequence?

❒ What accountability measures will be used?

- Group accountability

- Individual accountability

concerning the task. For example, if they are working together to analyze the structure of an argument put forward by an author, provide them with a rubric describing what you're looking for in the final product that they will be producing. Younger children can benefit from task cards that describe each step in detail. Many students benefit from timelines as well. Multi-step tasks can be broken down into units of time to give a pair or group another way of monitoring their progress.

Accountability

A common criticism of collaborative learning is that the distribution of labor may be uneven. However, this can only occur when there is a flawed accountability system in place. Authorities on this type of instructional arrangement recommend both group and individual accountability measures (Johnson, Johnson, Holubec, & Roy, 1984). This means that student learning should ideally be measured in two ways: first, through a group assessment linked to the completion of the task, and second, through an individual assessment designed to gauge each student's contributions to the effort. Considerations about how you will measure individual accountability should be taken into account when you are building the task itself. Below are some structures for collaborative work that can provide built-in accountability measures.

A common criticism of collaborative learning is that the distribution of labor may be uneven. However, this can only occur when there is a flawed accountability system.

- **A collaborative poster:** The teacher might assign each member of a group a different colored marker to use in the development of a collaborative poster. In this way, the different colors serve as evidence of each member's contributions.
- **Literature circles:** In literature circles, students' notes typically highlight each member's contributions. It is also common, for instance, to use assigned roles when students are first learning the literature circle format (e.g., the discussion director, vocabulary enricher, etc.). The notes students create during their literature circle meeting can be organized to mirror the roles they are using. As the groups become more proficient, the distinction between the roles can be faded.
- **A discussion roundtable:** Another way to ensure group and individual accountability is through the use of a discussion roundtable. Students can simply fold a

Video 4.7

Students collaborating to learn content.
resources.corwin.com/ rigorousreadingtx

Figure 4.3 Discussion Roundtable

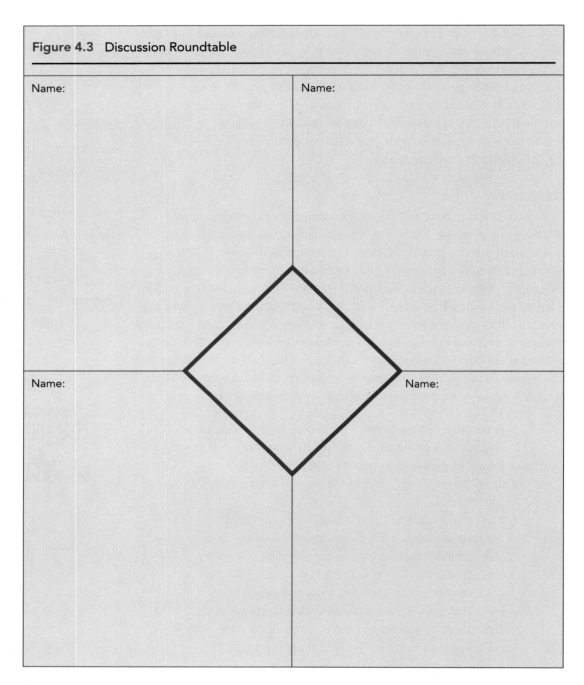

piece of paper like the one in Figure 4.3. As they read a selected piece of text, they take notes in the upper-left quadrant. They then take turns discussing the text and recording the content that their peers share in the other quadrants. At the end of the conversation they can summarize their understanding of the text, identify the theme, or ask questions (depending on the task assigned the teacher) in the area in the center.

Students need time every day, in every class, to practice their collaborative conversations.

Student self-assessments are also useful when developing collaborative learning skills in the classroom. Students in secondary school are developmentally more capable of distinguishing between the work of the group and their own role in influencing group dynamics. They can complete an individual feedback sheet that gives them an opportunity to reflect on their own contributions and set goals for future collaborative partnerships. These are completed and turned in with the written work. A combination of encouraging students' goal setting and providing them with opportunities for self-evaluation has been shown to improve academic achievement (Schunk, 1998). An example of an individual feedback sheet for older students appears in Figure 4.4. An individual self-assessment for younger students appears in Figure 4.5.

By establishing favorable conditions for collaborative learning, the peer-led portion of class time will run smoothly and result in rewarding exchanges among students. Keep in mind that these collaborative skills should be taught first, through modeling, and that students should then receive feedback about their performance in collaborative tasks. As students become more proficient in the curriculum and self-assessment, they will be prepared to apply them to collaborative learning situations.

When teachers use collaborative learning to help students meet the demands of accessing complex text, the most obvious implication it will have on their instruction will relate to the use of time. Students need time every day, in every class, to practice their collaborative conversations. That's not to say teachers should simply turn over their classrooms to students to talk, but rather that there should be expectations established for student-to-student interaction and that there should be an understanding that students will be held accountable for these interactions.

Figure 4.4   Individual Self-Assessment for Older Students

Name: _____   Date: _____

Name of Project/Assignment: _____

Evaluate your contributions to the collaborative task you completed. Read each statement and circle the number in the column on the right that represents *your* role best.

1 = never

2 = rarely

3 = sometimes

4 = usually

5 = always

I contributed ideas to the discussion.	1	2	3	4	5
I listened to the ideas of others.	1	2	3	4	5
I asked questions.	1	2	3	4	5
I located resources when needed.	1	2	3	4	5
I completed my tasks on time.	1	2	3	4	5
I did my fair share of the work.	1	2	3	4	5

My best contribution to this task was

The next time I work in a group, I will improve on

Based on my assessment, I would give myself a grade of _____.

Figure 4.5 Self-Assessment for Younger Students

Name: _____ Date: _____

Type of Work I Did: _____

Partners' Names: _____

How do I rate my work?

	Always	Sometimes	Not Yet
I asked questions.			
I listened when others talked.			
I did a fair share of the work.			
I used ideas from other people, not just my own.			
I was prepared to work.			

Video 4.8

Teacher facilitates a discussion as practice for students' collaborative work.

resources.corwin.com/ rigorousreadingtx

▶ Accessing Complex Texts Requires Student-to-Student Interaction

As we have noted, students must learn to interact with one another and the text if they are going to demonstrate proficiency with complex texts. There are a number of different ways to accomplish this, some of which have already been discussed, such as using literature circles and discussion roundtables. The remainder of this chapter provides a review of two additional collaborative learning structures that teachers can use to provide students opportunities to engage with their peers as they access complex texts: reciprocal teaching and collaborative strategic reading.

Reciprocal Teaching

As groups of students read and talk about what they read, they learn more. One structure for facilitating student reading and discussion is reciprocal teaching (Palincsar & Brown, 1984). During reciprocal teaching conversations, students assume practice with a specific comprehension strategy:

- Predicting
- Questioning
- Summarizing
- Clarifying

As they read, they pause periodically and talk about what they are reading. In some cases, they change roles each time they talk. In other cases, they practice the same role throughout the reading. It's important to note that reciprocal teaching groups do not have to consist of four students; students can share a role, or a student can have more than one role. The point of reciprocal teaching is to encourage reading, and deep understanding, of a piece of text. For example, during their discussion of immigration, as part of a unit on industrialization in America, students in Javier Vaca's U.S. history class engaged in reciprocal teaching when they encountered complex texts. Part of the conversation of one group highlights the learning that occurred:

Marco: So, I have a question. What does it mean "push and pull"? What does that have to do with immigration?

Daisy: I think that they're saying that there were things that pushed the immigrants out of their home countries. Like, for example, some people weren't respected because of their religion.

Alexis: Yeah, and then some people were pushed out because they didn't have enough money. That was gonna be part of my summary, because they are saying that when people cannot afford to live in a place, they want to look for a new opportunity.

Uriel: That's the pull, right? Because the U.S. was a place where people could go to get a better life, and make enough money to take care of their family. So, I'll make a prediction. I predict that the next section will tell why that didn't work, because we still have a lot of poverty here, so it couldn't have all worked.

Vanessa: I remember that part where it said that the immigrants thought that "the streets were paved with gold." See, right here [pointing to a place in the text], but they weren't. They were just normal streets, but that was a pull, to think that the U.S. had so much money that they put gold on the street.

The point of reciprocal teaching is to encourage reading, and deep understanding, of a piece of text.

Collaborative Strategic Reading

Collaborative strategic reading (CSR) is a technique used by small groups of heterogeneously grouped students to read and comprehend text (Klinger & Vaughn, 1998). Typically used in groups of five, it is well suited for use with informational text, although it can be used in conjunction with narrative text as well. When using this technique, a text is divided into smaller sections so that the group stops from time to time to discuss what they know so far and what is confusing or unclear. The strength of this approach lies in the use of cooperative learning principles to practice sound comprehension strategies. The following four strategies, which are described in the sections that follow, are used by the group to understand the text:

- Preview
- Click and clunk
- Get the gist
- Wrap up

By creating prediction questions, students can begin to anticipate the information they may encounter during the reading.

Each of these strategies is taught and practiced in a whole-class context until students are able to use them without teacher support. A study of CSR in fourth-grade classrooms found that students who had been carefully taught each of the strategies focused the majority of their talk (65%) on the content of the reading, and another 25% on the procedural aspects of CSR; in contrast, only 2% of their talk was off task (Klinger, Vaughn, & Schumm, 1998).

Before the Reading: Preview

This step is performed before the reading. Students discuss what they already know about the topic of the reading and make predictions about what may be learned in the reading. By creating prediction questions, students can begin to anticipate the information they may encounter during the reading.

During the Reading: Click and Clunk

Click is the term used by the authors to describe smooth reading that makes sense to the student, much like the hum of a well-oiled machine. On the other hand, *clunk* describes the times when a reader encounters an unfamiliar word or concept. Together, clicks and clunks represent self-monitoring behaviors used by fluent readers. The clunks signal to the readers that other strategies for resolving comprehension problems are needed. After noticing that a problem has occurred, the reader can

- *reread* the sentence or paragraph;
- *read ahead* until the end of the sentence or paragraph;
- *analyze* the word for familiar affixes or root words; or
- *ask* his or her partner what it means.

During CSR, students read a passage from the text then discuss their clunks. Using their collective knowledge, they clarify each other's understanding of the word or concept in question.

During the Reading: Get the Gist

At the end of each section of the passage, students summarize the main ideas and important facts. Like prediction and self-monitoring, summarizing is a comprehension behavior used by fluent readers (Brown & Day, 1983). Both click and clunk and get the gist are repeated several times until the entire reading has been completed.

After the Reading: Wrap Up

Once the group has finished with the reading, they revisit the predictions they made to check for accuracy. They also generate questions and answers that focus on the main ideas and important facts.

Students are initially assigned roles in CSR so that the discussion will flow more smoothly, and in time, these distinctions are faded as groups become more proficient with the process. These roles include the following:

Like prediction and self-monitoring, summarizing is a comprehension behavior used by fluent readers.

- **Leader:** makes sure the strategies are used and seeks help from the teacher when needed
- **Clunk expert:** leads discussion on how to figure out unknown words or concepts
- **Announcer:** makes sure everyone has a chance to participate
- **Reporter:** shares the group's work during the "share" portion of the language arts workshop
- **Timer:** monitors the time so the group can complete the task during collaborative learning

A group of third-grade students used CSR with the picture book *Stick Out Your Tongue!* (Bonsignore, 2001). An excerpt of the book read,

> Moths and butterflies use their tongues like straws to suck the sweet nectar from flowers.
>
> The tongue of an insect like a moth or butterfly is quite different from the tongues of other animals. These insects have a proboscis, a mouthpart that extends out and forms a long, thin tube much like a tiny straw. The moth or butterfly sticks the proboscis deep into the heart of the flower blossom and sucks the sweet nectar. One moth in Madagascar has a proboscis that is nine inches long! That's about as long as your mom's foot! (p. 3)

Ting, the leader of the group, asked everyone to read the page, then called on Kimberly, the clunk expert, to start the discussion about difficult vocabulary. "Did anyone have a clunk—a tricky word?"

Gaining access to complex text requires collaborative conversations because students need to talk about texts and make meaning with their peers.

"I had a bunch of them," said Marvin. Alicia, the announcer, reminded him to pick one so that everyone would have a turn. "I pick this word, then," said Marvin, pointing to *proboscis*. "I don't even know how to say it!"

Kimberly followed. "I had trouble with that one, too. Let's look at the list to see how we can figure it out. Let's reread the sentence." After all of them finished rereading, Marvin exclaimed, "There it is! It's 'a mouthpart that extends out and forms a long, thin tube.' It's right here in the picture." He points to the illustration of a moth using his proboscis to suck nectar from the center of a daisy.

"The illustrator even drew a picture of a boy drinking from a straw to remind us of how it works," offered Wilfredo. The leader continued the conversation, and the group discussed *blossom* (Marvin knew this word), *nectar* (they made a connection to *nectarine* and decided it was something sweet), and *Madagascar* (they used context clues to determine that it was a place, then consulted an atlas to pinpoint its location).

Wilfredo, the timer, reminded the group that they needed to "get the gist" if they were going to finish this passage. After discussing the main idea of the passage, they each wrote the following sentence in their journal:

Moths and butterflies use a proboscis to suck nectar from flowers.

After reading three more pages of the book together, the group had developed several summary sentences, which they incorporated into their written summary of the book.

▶ Summary

Gaining access to complex text requires collaborative conversations because students need to talk about texts and make meaning with their peers. In previous chapters, we explained how modeling academic discourse is a vital first step in fostering critical thinking. Students then begin to apply this discourse under the watchful eye of the teacher during close reading and scaffolded reading. But without opportunities to use this on their own during collaborative learning, students don't get the chance to practice how they "talk" to themselves as they read complex text independently. Collaborative learning, whether through literature circles, discussion roundtables, reciprocal teaching, or collaborative strategic reading, gives students the time they need to witness their own thinking and learn about the ideas of others.

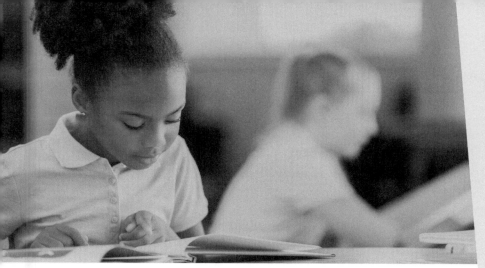

Access Point Four

An Independent Reading Staircase

Although it is independent reading time in Mrs. Garcia's fourth-grade class, it is far from silent. Several children are clustered in a comfortable corner of the room where rocking chairs and braided rugs offer an inviting space to get lost in a book. Others students are reading at their tables on iPads. Trisha and Leon are looking through a basket in the classroom library labeled *Gold Rush Books*, while Kaleem, Sonje, and Melissa are already reading. The pages of their books sprout sticky notes with handwritten annotations.

While most of the students are settling into their independent reading, Mrs. Garcia is seated at a small table in another corner of the room. To her left are a binder for her student reading conference notes and a stack of observation forms like the one in Figure 5.1. Patrice, a girl with braids and a quick smile, is discussing her book with her teacher.

"Tell me about the book you're reading, Patrice. What has happened so far?" asks Mrs. Garcia.

Figure 5.1 Reading Conference Form

Name: _____   Date: _____

Title and Author: _____

Retelling (check all that apply)

- ❐ discusses important events
- ❐ offers salient details
- ❐ uses evidence from the text to support retelling
- ❐ states opinion
- ❐ provides textual support for opinion
- ❐ needs prompts to expand answers

Notes:

Oral Reading Fluency

- ❐ reads accurately
- ❐ fluently, in long phrases
- ❐ choppy, in short phrases
- ❐ word by word
- ❐ with expression
- ❐ flat and without expression

Notes:

Goals for Next Meeting

"It's really good!" offers Patrice.

> I'm reading *Seeds of Hope* [Gregory, 2001], and it's about a girl named Susanna who is traveling on a ship to get to Oregon. Her mom died on the ship, and her dad lost all their money. Now they're going to go to California because they heard about gold.

This novel, told in diary form, has been a popular choice among many of the students in the class during the last few weeks.

After asking a few more questions to confirm Patrice's comprehension, Mrs. Garcia asks her to read a passage that was meaningful to her. Patrice chooses the journal entry when Susanna's father tells her they will be going to California instead of Oregon. While Patrice reads, Mrs. Garcia makes notes about Patrice's reading fluency and her use of expression. Mrs. Garcia then asks Patrice about observations she has made during the reading. Patrice turns to the section of the book about when Susanna's father tells her he is going to be a gold miner, not a doctor.

> I was thinking about another book I read this year called *Riding Freedom* [Ryan, 1999]. Susanna reminds me of Charley in *Riding Freedom* because she has to learn how to rely on herself when her parents aren't there for her anymore.

A guiding principle of the Texas English Language Arts and Reading Standards is that students should achieve a level of independence that makes it possible for them to express their own thoughts and ideas and to understand the thoughts and ideas of others.

As their reading conference draws to an end, Mrs. Garcia and Patrice develop a goal for Patrice to look for historical connections since they are studying the California Gold Rush in social studies. With that, Patrice leaves the table with her book in hand. Looking back over her shoulder, Patrice remarks, "I'll let you know what happens next!"

A guiding principle of the Texas English Language Arts and Reading Standards is that students should achieve a level of independence that makes it possible for them to express their own thoughts and ideas and to understand the thoughts and ideas of others. In the language of the standards, students "self-select text and interact independently with text for increasing periods of time." In part, access to complex texts comes from engaging in deliberate and sustained practice in reading.

Marie Clay (2001) refers to this as "the high demand from the first days of school for children to read and write texts according to their competencies but always as independently as possible" (p. 48). After all, as educators, our intent is to develop a set of skills in each learner that ultimately can be used outside the presence of the teacher. Like all aspects of learning, each student's ability to engage in independent tasks is fostered through explicit instruction.

An important advantage of developing independent learners is that the teacher can then use his or her time to support the efforts of individual students.

An important advantage of developing independent learners is that the teacher can then use his or her time to support the efforts of individual students. Within every class, there exist some students who need more specialized teacher supports; as well, every student, regardless of achievement level, needs personal contact with the teacher. As busy classroom teachers know, this can happen on a consistent basis only when all the students know how to work collaboratively and independently. A powerful practice for making contact with each student is known as *conferring*. Teachers confer with students through rich conversations about their reading practices.

This chapter focuses on the roles of students and teachers as they access complex texts during independent learning. While students work independently to apply the literacy skills and strategies they have been taught during modeling, close reading, scaffolded reading instruction, and collaborative learning, teachers are conferring with students individually to engage them in important conversations about their learning.

The Goals of Independent Learning

It seems as if the practice of having students working quietly and independently on individual tasks is as old a concept as school itself. Many of us have memories of toiling away on worksheets while the teacher walked up and down the aisles. Rarely were any words exchanged, other than those pertaining to simple questions about the assignment at hand. When completed, these worksheets were turned in to be graded. Rarely did we understand how any of these worksheets connected to our learning. The goal instead seemed to be to complete the workbook or the pile of dittos in our folders.

There are several drawbacks associated with this approach to independent work. For one, the work completed independently may focus

Video 5.1

Doug discusses independent learning.
resources.corwin.com/ rigorousreadingtx

on many repetitions of the same isolated skills, leading to disengagement and boredom. This is especially true for struggling readers who will sometimes focus on getting the assignment done rather than on the intended learning outcomes that were built into the lesson design (Anderson, Brubaker, Alleman-Brooks, & Duffy, 1985). For example, envision the student who completes a spelling assignment of writing each word 10 times by instead writing each letter in a vertical column of 10 until the entire word is completed. After completing the list, the student is no closer to remembering how to spell the word than when she began. When we talk about independent learning, we are not referring to activities like worksheets intended to keep students quiet and occupied. The goal of independent learning is to empower students to develop self-regulation skills, increase their sense of competence, and set goals for themselves. Below, we discuss these three goals in greater detail.

Self-Regulation

Independent learning provides students with opportunities to self-regulate—to manage their time, monitor their progress, and solve problems. In their study of third graders, Stright and Supplee (2002) found that students were more likely to ask for help and monitor their progress during independent learning when they had been taught how to do so. Good and Brophy (2003) consider self-regulation to be an essential component of the curriculum:

> Students cannot learn self-regulation and self-control if the teacher does all of the alerting, accountability, and so on. They need to be taught to manage time (we have fifteen minutes to finish a task) and to define their own work and procedures (what is the critical problem—how else might the problem be approached?) This appropriate management necessitates that rules and structures—the scaffolding–be progressively altered to encourage more responsibility for self-control. (p. 137)

When students have daily opportunities to engage in meaningful independent learning, they not only apply literacy skills and strategies but also develop the ability to regulate and monitor their pace of work and hone their problem-solving skills.

A powerful practice for making contact with each student is known as conferring. Teachers confer with students through rich conversations about their reading practices.

Competence

In addition to helping students self-regulate, independent learning provides them with a chance to develop a sense of competence. The concept of competence hinges on a learner's perception of her abilities and on her understanding of the effort needed to accomplish a task. While many speak of the importance of self-esteem in the learning process, it is *competenc*e that really contributes to a learner's self-esteem. It is through a sense of competence that self-esteem is built. This, in turn, increases motivation, because we are motivated to do those things we know we do well. When students have the opportunity to explore and experience their own competence through independent learning, their self-efficacy improves, and they begin to believe that learning is under their control (Yeager & Dweck, 2012).

When we talk about independent learning, we are not referring to activities like worksheets intended to keep students quiet and occupied.

Goal Setting

A final positive aspect of independent learning is that it allows students to gain experience at setting and achieving goals. Alexander and Jetton (2000, p. 297) describe students as possessing one or more of the following goal orientations that serve to propel or inhibit their learning.

- **Performance goals:** Students who view learning through this lens are interested in teacher recognition and good grades. The extrinsic rewards of the task become the goal for completing the work.
- **Mastery goals:** Students with this orientation are interested in the content of the task and the opportunity to expand their own knowledge base.
- **Work-avoidant goals:** Some students are primarily interested in completing the task with the least amount of effort necessary.

All students are motivated by a combination of these goals to varying degrees. However, it is important to recognize that all of these orientations exist and that the second category—that of the mastery goals—is the one that teachers should aim to cultivate. Independent learning provides teachers with the perfect opportunity to make this happen, as this is a format in which students will experience many opportunities to set their own goals and monitor their progress toward attaining them. In addition, the practice of independent learning provides teachers with opportunities to monitor their students—through conferring—throughout the learning process.

▶ Accessing Complex Texts Requires Wide, Independent Reading

One way to ensure that students read in class is to provide them with time to read. Unlike silent sustained reading in which students read texts of their own choosing, independent reading constrains students' choices, and they read increasingly complex texts. For example, earth science teacher Adam Renick provides 10 minutes each day for his students to independently read complex texts about the content they are studying. Mr. Renick notes, "Scientists read every day as part of their job, and I want my students to have that same experience." Reading widely builds background knowledge and vocabulary, which is essential for strengthening disciplinary knowledge. Students can't draw on personal experiences alone when learning about the physical, social, and biological world, particularly as the content grows more technical in middle school. They must read complex texts that develop their knowledge. There is evidence that when students are provided with time for independent reading of content-area-aligned texts, their academic performance improves (Fisher, Ross, & Grant, 2010).

Students were more likely to ask for help and monitor their progress during independent learning when they had been taught how to do so.

To understand complex texts, students must master content-area knowledge. They should view reading as a means of gaining such knowledge. Stated a different way, knowledge cannot be built simply by telling students what they need to know. They need to see texts as an important source of information. Thoughtfully chosen independent reading materials afford students with opportunities to (1) apply what they have been taught about comprehension and (2) build their knowledge about the topics they are studying. It's really like climbing a staircase. It takes you to a new level, but that doesn't mean that you have to always be at that level. The staircase represents an effort but a goal that can be accomplished.

This staircase has to be built over years, as well as over units of study and phases of instruction. The texts selected for independent reading on a given day should be complex, but perhaps not as complex as those used during close reading or scaffolded reading that occurs on the same day. However, there should be a steady, forward progression in the complexity of texts used in independent reading and collaborative conversations; this progression should mirror the trajectory of increasing text complexity followed when engaging in close readings.

Independent reading is important because students need time to try on the strategies they have been learning. Thus, the practice of independent reading is connected with the modeling and scaffolded instruction students have received. The effectiveness of independent reading is rooted in two concepts: increasing reading volume and developing positive reading attitudes.

When students have the opportunity to explore and experience their own competence through independent learning, their self-efficacy improves, and they begin to believe that learning is under their control.

Reading Volume

Reading volume is a measure of the amount of reading a learner engages in both in school and at home. Stanovich (1986) examined the relationship between students' volume of outside reading and their ability to read. This study confirmed what many teachers had always known—the more reading students do, the better their reading becomes. A related study compared students' standardized test scores in reading and the amount of outside reading they did. As in the earlier study, the results indicated that there was a strong correlation between reading volume and achievement (Anderson, Wilson, & Fielding, 1988). A table of the results can be seen in Figure 5.2. These and similar studies spurred educators' interest in carving out a portion of the school day during which students could read independently for an extended period of time.

Positive Reading Attitudes

In addition to exploring the connection between reading and achievement, studies have demonstrated the importance of positive reading attitudes. Concern over this topic is well founded because positive student attitudes toward reading decline during the late elementary years, especially among boys (Kush & Watkins, 1996). A large-scale study based on national testing results suggested that students who had positive attitudes toward reading (described as *engaged readers*) outperformed older, disengaged readers (Campbell, Voekl, & Donahue, 1997). An analysis of fourth graders' results on the same test revealed that engaged readers from low-income backgrounds outperformed disengaged readers from

Figure 5.2 Relationship Between Achievement and Independent Reading

Percentile Rank	Minutes of Reading per Day (Books)	Words Read per Year
98	65.0	4,358,000
90	21.1	1,823,000
80	14.2	1,146,000
70	9.6	622,000
60	6.5	432,000
50	4.6	282,000
40	3.2	200,000
30	1.8	106,000
20	0.7	21,000
10	0.1	8,000
2	0.0	0

Source: Adapted from Anderson et al. (1988). Used with permission.

higher socioeconomic backgrounds (Guthrie, Schafer, & Huang, 2001). These positive attitudes toward reading are developed through

- clear learning goals;
- texts that relate to a student's personal experiences;
- support from the teacher on making choices;
- texts with interesting topics;
- instruction in reading strategies;
- opportunities to collaborate with other students;
- a positive environment that is not driven by extrinsic rewards;

- evaluation that provides feedback on progress, rather than tests of knowledge;
- personal connections to the teacher; and
- cohesive instruction. (Guthrie & Wigfield, 2000)

A student discusses SSR.
*resources.corwin.com/
rigorousreadingtx*

Differences Between SSR and Independent Reading

There are some differences between sustained silent reading (SSR) and independent reading, although both of them have their place in the classroom. In particular, they differ in terms of overall purpose, book selection and access, accountability, and roles of the student and teacher. A summary of these differences can be seen in Figure 5.3.

Goals and Purpose. The primary goal of SSR is to develop positive student attitudes toward reading and to encourage students to view reading as a recreational activity. On the other hand, the goal of independent reading is to provide time for practice of skills and strategies taught in other phases of instruction.

Book Selection. In SSR, the student makes the ultimate decision about what he or she will read. The teacher provides guidance and information about choosing books that are a "good fit," but a student is never discouraged from reading a particular book. In independent reading, the teacher has more influence over what will be read because the text should connect to the content being taught. In addition, the independent reading text should build the reading prowess of students, taking them up another step on their staircase to accessing complex texts.

Book Access. During independent reading, a narrow range of texts are made available because the purpose is to practice using a skill or strategy. In SSR, students have access to and read a wide range of materials, including nontraditional texts like comic books, magazines, and web-based information.

Accountability. During independent reading, students spend some of their time completing reading logs, graphic organizers, précis writing, and written reflections about the reading. In SSR, nonaccountability is the hallmark. Students simply read.

Figure 5.3   Differences Between SSR and Independent Reading

	Sustained Silent Reading	Independent Reading
Goals and purpose	• Reading for pleasure	• Building mastery through practice
Book selection	• Student choice with a wide range of genres and levels	• Constrained choice of increasingly complex texts
Accountability	• No records kept	• Logs and reflections are essential
What are students doing?	• Reading quietly	• Reading and writing reflections • Conferring with teacher
What is the teacher doing?	• Brief book talk • Reading quietly	• Conferring with students • Observing • Assessing
Follow-up activity	• Students can volunteer to briefly talk about a book; this is not always a part of an SSR session	• Students discuss their reading. The discussion is related to the purpose set at the beginning of the session

Student's Role. During SSR, students read until the end of the time allotted, then transition to the next activity. During independent reading, students may be reading, writing about their reading, or conferring with the teacher about their reading.

Teacher's Role. During SSR, the teacher reads to provide an adult model of recreational reading. During independent reading, the teacher is conferring with students, assessing and observing while students read.

Follow-Up Activities. In SSR, students may be invited to share a book they are reading. However, this is never a requirement, and students are free to volunteer or not. In independent reading, a sharing phase is included at the end of each reading period. The discussions students engage in during this sharing phase are based on the assignment that was given to them before the independent reading began.

One of the goals of independent reading is to provide students with an opportunity to write about thoughts, ideas, and evidence that connect to their reading.

Students Respond During Independent Reading

One of the goals of independent reading is to provide students with an opportunity to write about thoughts, ideas, and evidence that connect to their reading. These written responses are usually brief in nature, and teachers can use a variety of tools with their students to help them organize their thoughts as they are writing. We have included several samples of these tools at the end of this chapter to provide you with examples of reading logs and comment cards for a range of grade levels.

Comment Cards

Students use these simple note taking frameworks to jot down thoughts and ideas related to the strategies and skills they are practicing or the content they are learning. This is an early form of annotation for students who are just beginning to learn this skill. A sample comment card appears in Figure 5.4.

For example, Aida Allen asked her fifth graders to look for evidence of foreshadowing during independent reading. Jeremy reviewed the previous chapters he had already read and wrote several notes on his comment card about *Frindle* (Clements, 1996; see Figure 5.5).

Sticky Notes

As students become more adept at making notes as they are reading—and if they are not allowed to annotate directly on the text—they can move from comment cards to sticky notes. These small notes can be positioned to "underline" important passages students encounter. A challenge of using sticky notes is teaching students how to use them with an economy of words. Learners who have been accustomed to writing on 8-1/2″ × 11″ sheets of paper may attempt to crowd too many words onto these small notes. It is useful for them to have a bank of simple annotations available to help them abbreviate their thoughts while still preserving meaning.

Video 5.3

Teachers talk about the use of independent reading.

resources.corwin.com/ rigorousreadingtx

Figure 5.4 Comment Cards

Comment Card	Comment Card	Comment Card
During today's reading, I am looking for:	During today's reading, I am looking for:	During today's reading, I am looking for:
I found examples on:	*I found examples on:*	*I found examples on:*
Pg. _____	Pg. _____	Pg. _____
Pg. _____	Pg. _____	Pg. _____
Pg. _____	Pg. _____	Pg. _____
Pg. _____	Pg. _____	Pg. _____

Figure 5.5   Jeremy's Comment Card

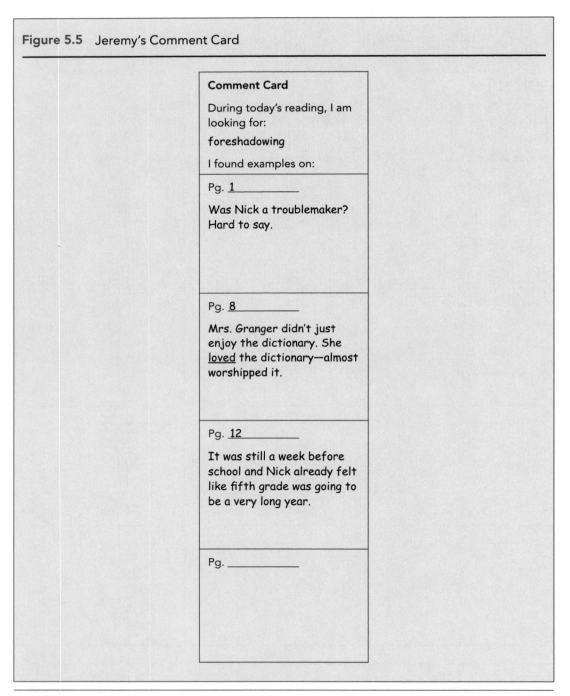

Comment Card

During today's reading, I am looking for:

foreshadowing

I found examples on:

Pg. _1_____

Was Nick a troublemaker? Hard to say.

Pg. _8_____

Mrs. Granger didn't just enjoy the dictionary. She <u>loved</u> the dictionary—almost worshipped it.

Pg. _12_____

It was still a week before school and Nick already felt like fifth grade was going to be a very long year.

Pg. _____

Reflection Journals

Independent readers not only read for meaning; they also need to reflect on and discuss their readings with others. To support their discussions, students need to make notes and write down their thoughts and observations. The purpose for reading should be established at the beginning of the independent reading time, with appropriate instruction about what to look for in the reading. Many teachers find that instructing students to begin notes from each reading session on a new page of a reflection journal (complete with date, title, and relevant page numbers) is helpful for keeping students organized. These response journal entries can address a range of topics, but generally offer students the opportunities to engage in a meaningful transaction with the text. Students can then draw from the content of these reflection journals during class discussions to provide evidence from the texts they are reading; these journals are also read by the teacher.

There is a transaction that occurs between the text and the reader that makes each text–reader relationship unique.

Readers make meaning at the word level through understanding the vocabulary, and at the sentence and paragraph levels through understanding how ideas are crafted by the author to tell a story or forward a position on a topic. But readers also make meaning through their own transactions with the text. They activate their background knowledge to determine the veracity of the text—"Could this happen?" Finally, they analyze the text for its usefulness to them—"What did I learn from this text?" In other words, the words on the page do not simply lie there waiting to be consumed without analysis by the reader. Instead, there is a transaction that occurs between the text and the reader that makes each text–reader relationship unique. This is why, for example, one person can love a book while another considers it a complete waste of time.

Those transactions form the basis for reader response theory (Rosenblatt, 1938/1995). Reader response theory suggests that all reading experiences can be described as a balance between efferent (information-seeking) and aesthetic (emotional) responses. It is important to note that one is not more valued than another, but rather that each reading experience can be represented on a continuum between these two response types. For example, a reader's response to Robert Frost's poem "Stopping By Woods on a Snowy Evening" may be primarily aesthetic as the reader enjoys how Frost crafts his words and meter. However, there is still likely to be an efferent component as the reader constructs his understanding of the woods. At the other extreme, a reader's response to the book *How Animals Shed Their Skin* (Tatham, 2002) may be primarily efferent as he or she looks for information about leopard frogs. Even then, there is likely to be an aesthetic response as well when they view the weird and wonderful animals in the photographs. Although it is not necessary to teach students these terms (we shudder at the thought of a second grader offering, "I would like to make an aesthetic response to *Madeline*"), it is important that they have many opportunities to explore their transactions with the texts they are reading. As they gain insight into the way they are interacting with the texts, they will become conscious of their learning and build their metacognitive skills. In addition, this awareness will also feed into their ability to understand their levels of comprehension and self-monitor accordingly.

> *It should never be assumed that students know how to participate in rich discussions about a text. These skills should be explicitly taught so that students can begin to fully participate in this academic discourse.*

Students Talk About Texts

One of the desired outcomes of independent reading is that students will talk about the texts they are reading in collaborative conversations. These conversations can take place in small-group collaborative sessions or in a whole-class format. Providing students with time to share offers numerous benefits for readers. First, it is useful for oral language development at both the social and content levels. For English language learners in particular, it is an occasion to engage in academic language. Book discussions also provide opportunities for students to hone listening skills, particularly when they are encouraged to make connections to peers' comments rather than to direct their conversations to the teacher. These collaborative conversations are critical for helping students clarify their understanding of a text, ask questions, and deepen their understanding of complex texts. As with all aspects of instruction, it should never be assumed that students know how to participate in rich discussions about a text. Therefore, these skills should be explicitly taught so that students can begin to fully participate in this academic discourse.

An example of a collaborative conversation follows:

It is early October, and the students in Lisa Targas's first-grade classroom have been reading sequence stories to understand how an author can tell a tale that builds on the action. During her modeling, Ms. Targas used *Joseph Had a Little Overcoat* (Tayback, 1999) to chart the sequence of events that occurred as Joseph's coat became more worn and was converted into a jacket, vest, tie, patch, and button. During collaborative reading, students worked in small groups to create similar charts for *There Was an Old Lady Who Swallowed a Fly* (Tayback, 2007).

After multiple experiences with sequence texts, students were ready to read and discuss others during independent reading. Ms. Targas created a box full of books with stories that use sequence as a major feature. Students selected titles and created their own sequence charts, using a format similar to the one seen in Figure 5.6. While all of the students worked, Ms. Targas met with select individual students to confer about their work and also offered support for others who needed clarification on their reading.

When students finished reading and responding, they began to discuss the books they had chosen. Ms. Targas prompted,

> Remember to use your journals because that's where you have some of your good ideas written down. We're going to start by talking about the books you read. We paid attention to the sequences in our stories today so let's start there. Who would like to begin?

When students become more motivated to read, as is likely to occur when they are reading on a regular basis, it's more likely that they'll read at home.

The class discussed the plots of the stories and the sequences used. Stephanie remarked that her book, *The Napping House* (Wood, 2009), reminded her of the time the ceiling fan fell down in the living room one night and woke everyone in the house. As the students discussed the content, Ms. Targas made notes about students' performance. These notes serve as fodder for future instruction, including the individual conferences that she will have with her students.

▶ Increasing At-Home Reading

In addition to the independent reading time teachers provide students during the school day, to meet the standards and ensure that all students achieve at high levels, they have to engage in distributed practice outside of school. The correlational data about reading volume and achievement we presented earlier in this chapter was based on reading that students did outside of school. When students become more motivated to read, as is likely to occur when they are reading on a regular basis, it's more likely

Figure 5.6   Reading Journal Format for Sequence Stories

Title of book: _____   Author: _____

This book was about

The best part of this book was

One way the author could change this book is

Here's what happened in the text (use pictures and words)

1	2	3
4	**5**	**6**

that they'll read at home. There are a few things that teachers can do to encourage students to increase their at-home reading volume, and one of them we have already discussed, which is to provide students opportunities to talk about what they are reading during school. In addition to these very valuable discussions about texts, the following three actions can help:

Access. If there is little to read in your house, you're less likely to read. To raise the volume of reading outside the school day, students must have access to texts. There have been a number of efforts to "flood" students with things to read (e.g., Elley, 2000) to address the need for students to have access to reading materials. The International Literacy Association (ILA) recommends a minimum of seven books per student in the class. That would mean that a classroom library for a group of 28 students would need nearly 200 texts for students to read. In addition to classroom libraries, school libraries can be additional resources that provide students with access to texts. ILA (2000) recommends a ratio of 20 books per child for school libraries.

However, Newman's (2017) study of 15 childcare centers in an urban area serving 501 children demonstrated that there was little impact from a book flood alone, noting, "the results of our study suggest that access to such books may be necessary, but it was clearly insufficient to enhance early literacy skills" (p. 18).

Choice. When students have choice over their reading materials, they are more likely to read. Choice is key to motivation and academic independence (Schunk, Meece, & Pintrich, 2013). Teachers can assign reading for students to do, especially during class time, when scaffolding can be provided. But to increase reading volume, teachers have to expand the amount of choice students have in what they read. Students who have opportunities to choose their own books develop elaborate strategies for selecting books and are more likely to become intrinsically motivated readers. In their studies of reading motivation, Guthrie et al. (2007) noted, "students expressed that they like both making their own book choices, as well as having close, trusted others choose books for them" (p. 306). Choice does not necessarily mean "read whatever you want," but it might. For example, students could be provided a choice of texts based on a theme or essential question under investigation. Or students could be invited to continue reading their independent-reading text. Or students might be offered free range to read what they want.

Book Talks and "Blessing Books." When trusted others make recommendations about a text, potential readers are more likely to read it. To promote wide reading outside the school day, students need recommendations from others. Book talks conducted by trusted adults and peers can spur voluntary reading. Gambrell calls this "blessed books" (Marinak & Gambrell, 2016) and suggests that teachers talk about several books that readers in the class might enjoy. These books are then placed on a special shelf, face forward if possible, for students to select. Wozniak (2011) conducted an intervention to increase voluntary reading among sixth graders in her school using book talks to anchor the program. Teachers spent 10 minutes three times a week introducing books to their students. Students were also provided with 15 to 20 minutes of unrestricted reading time with any book in the classroom, including short partner discussions. In this investigation, "There were no guidelines, so their discussions took on different forms" such as discussing what was happening in the book or making recommendations (p. 20). Students were free to talk about their reading rather than be restricted by school-bound book reports that are dutifully delivered but rarely deeply felt (White & Greenfield, 1995). The results of the intervention included positive changes in measures of reading attitude, self-efficacy, and reading outside of school.

The purpose of a reading conference is determined by the teacher and student together because the conversation should be a give-and-take of questions and ideas.

Students can "bless" books, too. As Hudson (2016) notes, primary students can conduct peer-led book talks, promoting interest while also learning about one another as readers. Hudson modeled book talks herself, introducing a few titles each day, and included some specifics about the title, name of the author, and a brief description of characters and plot. Most importantly, she added recommendations. Within a short time, her first-grade students were leading book talks each week on a rotating basis.

▶ Accessing Complex Texts Requires Conferring

When students are reading or writing independently, the teacher can use some of this time to meet individually with students. Conferring provides the teacher with an excellent assessment opportunity. These conferences allow the teacher to gauge the progress of each student, clarify information, and provide feedback for next steps. In addition, teachers keep records of these conversations for later reflection about individual student progress. These conferences are brief in nature (a few minutes or so) and can be used as a follow up to inform further scaffolded instruction. Teachers usually average between three and five student conferences per independent reading session.

Effective conferences include four elements. Because each conference event is short, these elements come into play very quickly. When conferring, the student and teacher use the learner's work as evidence. The teacher focuses on only one or two points during a single session. A helpful sequence for a conference is as follows:

- **Inquiry:** The teacher begins by conversing with the student about his or her work. The goal is to assess the student on one literacy focus topic per session.
- **Decisions:** Based on the evidence culled from the opening conversation, the teacher rapidly makes a decision about what should be taught next.
- **Instruction:** The teacher provides a minute or two of procedural, literary, or strategic instruction to help the student move to the next level of independent learning, and the student attempts the work with teacher support.
- **Recordkeeping:** The teacher makes anecdotal notes about the main points of the conference.

The notes generated from these conferences will be consulted again later for further instructional and evaluative decisions. It is not uncommon for teachers to customize their conferring forms to meet the unique needs of their classrooms. However, a basic format for a conference appears in Figure 5.7.

The goal of a reading conference is to engage a student in a conversation about the book he or she is reading. The purpose of a reading conference is determined by the teacher and student together because the conversation should be a give-and-take of questions and ideas. In any case, the student and teacher should use both the text and reading journal during the conversation. The scenario at the beginning of this chapter is a reading conference. Useful goals for a reading conference include the following:

- Discuss something in the text.
- Ask about areas of confusion.

Video 5.4

Asking Children to Use Textual Evidence in Kindergarten.
resources.corwin.com/ rigorousreadingtx

Figure 5.7 Overview Form for Conferences

Name	Date	Type of Conference	Topic Discussed	Next Meeting	Goal for Next Meeting

Types of conferences:
    RC: reading conference
    WC: writing conference
    O: other (specify)

- Discuss the author's purpose or craft.
- Review the student's list of books read.
- Set reading goals together.

▶ Summary

Independent reading is a time when students get to practice applying what they have been learning during other parts of the instructional day or unit of study. Typically, students read a book that has been selected by the teacher because it features opportunities for them to use or draw from techniques or content they have already been learning. Students may respond in a reading journal and then use these notes to participate in discussions with other students. Teachers and students confer about independent reading and writing. The goal of these conferences is to engage students in an individual conversation about their work. A useful sequence for teachers to use during a conference is to first inquire, then make decisions about the immediate needs of the student. Teachers should be sure to note important details of the conference for next time and to end the session with a goal that the student can accomplish. When students read independently and confer with their teachers about the texts they are reading, they begin to access complex texts in new ways, ways that build the habits necessary for them to read for meaning in college and throughout their careers.

When students read independently and confer with their teachers about the texts they are reading, they begin to access complex texts in new ways.

istock.com/SolStock

Access Point Five

Assessing Students' Understanding

Internet searches often yield surprising results. Recently, Nancy searched one of her favorite sayings in preparation for a presentation she was doing about assessments: "You can't fatten sheep by weighing them." One of the results was an article from the April 1908 issue of the *Farm Journal* on early spring lambs. Among the advice to sheep farmers? Take care in apportioning their rations so as not to overfeed, provide healthy living conditions so they can grow, take careful measure of their progress, and keep this piece of wisdom in mind: "Study your sheep and know them not only as a flock but separately, and remember that they have an individuality as surely as your horse or cow" (Brick, 1908, p. 154).

Students are not sheep, of course, but our role as cultivators of young people has much in common with the role of a livestock farmer.

Without ways to look for patterns across students, formative assessments become a frustrating academic exercise.

As educators, we recognize the importance of a healthy learning climate, and we seek to create one each day. In addition, we apportion information so that students can act on their growing knowledge of the discipline. And we measure their progress throughout to see whether they are making expected gains. As part of effective practice, teachers routinely check for understanding through the learning process. This is most commonly accomplished by asking questions, analyzing tasks, and administering low-stakes quizzes to measure the extent to which students are acquiring new information and skills. But it's one thing to gather information (we're good at that); it's another to respond in meaningful ways and then plan for subsequent instruction. Without processes to provide students with solid feedback that yields deeper understanding, checking for understanding devolves into a game of "guess what's in the teacher's brain." And without ways to look for patterns across students, formative assessments become a frustrating academic exercise. Knowing both the flock and the individuals in it are the essential pieces of the puzzle for those in the cultivation business.

▶ Checking for Understanding

Before students can receive feedback, their peers or teachers need to know what they understood and did not understand. As we will discuss later, making instructional decisions based on student performance requires the collection of evidence. There are many ways to check for understanding that can guide the feedback students receive from peers or teachers. We see checking for understanding as a critical step in providing students access to complex texts, because analyzing the data can reveal areas of mastery and areas of confusion, allowing the teacher to take action.

"Did everybody get that?" says Mr. Unger. Rafael, a student in the class, thinks to himself, "No, I have no idea what you're talking about, but I'm not about to let everyone know that I'm confused." And so the game continues, with the teacher thinking he is checking for understanding and accepting the silence as an indicator that learning has occurred. In reality, despite quality instruction, Mr. Unger has no idea whether learning has or has not taken place.

How then could Mr. Unger check for understanding? What does quality checking for understanding look and sound like? Our analysis of classroom instruction and assessment suggests that there are several ways teachers can check for understanding, including the use of oral language, questioning, writing, projects and performances, and tests (Fisher & Frey, 2014). When teachers use these procedures, they know which students understand the content and which students need additional instruction. Checking for understanding, then, is an important part of a formative assessment system. Looking at student responses or student work informs the teacher, and that information can be acted upon to create better understanding. Importantly, checking for understanding has to occur throughout the lesson, at least every 5 to 10 minutes, if teachers want to maintain the rigor of the lesson while supporting student learning. Let's consider some of the common ways that teachers can check for understanding.

Oral Language

One effective way to check for understanding is through oral language: speaking and listening. When students are doing the talking, the teacher has a chance to assess understanding. There are a number of classroom structures that provide students an opportunity to talk, including think–pair–share, reciprocal teaching, literacy circles, discussion prompts, and Socratic seminars. For example, as Ms. Ramirez listens to her students discussing a book they are reading as part of their book club, she notices that they are not justifying their responses with evidence from the text. They are skilled at summarizing, but the lack of evidence in their discussions indicates a need to devote additional instructional time to this practice.

In addition to listening as students interact, retellings are a valuable way to check for understanding. Retellings provide the teacher with a glimpse into student thinking. For example, Mr. Bradford asked Jasmine to retell a section of video clip they had seen related to glacier formation and movement. As part of her retelling, Jasmine said, "The glaciers take a long time to develop. Well, really they grow like something alive even though they're not alive. They develop when it snows and the snow piles together. It changes to this special kind of ice, but before that, there is this in-between ice called firn." This retelling lets Mr. Bradford know that much of his teaching has stuck and that Jasmine is well on her way to understanding glaciers.

Questioning

Questioning, which can be done orally or in writing, is the most common way that teachers check for understanding. Unfortunately, not all questions are worthy of instructional time. To be useful, the initial questions teachers

Video 6.2

Teacher promotes students' reflection and metacognition after lesson.
resources.corwin.com/ rigorousreadingtx

ask should be planned in advance. Of course, additional questions that probe student understanding will come to mind during the interactions teachers have with students, but these initial questions form the expectations for student understanding. Less helpful questions are those we like to call "guess what's in the teacher's head." More formally known as Initiate–Respond–Evaluate or IRE (Cazden, 2001), this cycle privileges students who are willing to play the game. For example, when the teacher asks, "When do we use the FOIL rule?" Three or four students raise hands, and Tanya is selected to respond. Tanya says, "When you multiple binomials," to which the teacher responds, "Good." IRE is typically used with recall information and provides only a few students an opportunity to respond.

Instead, quality checking for understanding suggests that teachers need to ask questions that require more complex and critical thinking and that lots of students need to respond. There are a number of instructional routines that provide students with practice in questioning habits, such as ReQuest (Manzo, 1969), in which students read with a partner, taking turns asking and answering questions. As they practice, their teacher analyzes the types of questions being asked and the appropriateness of the answers. Over time (and with instruction and practice), students tire of the literal and recall questions and move toward more interesting questions that require synthesis and evaluation.

Another way to question in an inclusive way is through audience response systems. These can be as basic as 3- × 5-in. cards with answers on them that all students hold up to answer a question to as complex as handheld devices that allow each student to key in a response to a question. As an example of the former, as part of their opinionnaire in biology, students were provided with green and red cards, with *Yes* written on the green card and *No* written on the red card. As the teacher read each statement about the ecosystem, students held up one of their cards to indicate if they agreed or disagreed. A question about the impact of cleaning agents entering the water system through storm drains split the class, which provided the teacher information about where to focus the lesson. Audience responses systems, or "clickers," can be used to check for understanding of the whole class at once. For example, algebra teacher Aimee Chen poses a question and tells students to click in their responses then invites them to persuade one another about their choice before revealing the answer. She then engages them in reteaching. There is now an online version of audience response systems that rely on text messages from cell phones that can be found at www.polleverywhere.com.

Writing

When students are writing, they are thinking. In fact, it's nearly impossible to write and *not* think. That's why short writing-to-learn prompts are so effective for checking for understanding. It's important that the prompt be developed such that it provides teachers with information about student understanding. We are particularly taken with the RAFT writing prompt (Santa & Havens, 1995), which requires that students consider the **r**ole, **a**udience, **f**ormat, and **t**opic in their writing. There are, of course, many other writing prompts that can be used, but RAFT is flexible and teaches perspective. For example, after discussing sportsmanship in their physical education class, Mr. Davenport asks his students to respond to the following RAFT:

R   Bronze medal winner
A   Gold medal winner
F   Greeting card
T   Congratulations on your victory

Similarly, in a history classroom, students learn about the Gettysburg Address and discuss the role that this speech had in shaping US policy. To check their understanding about the address, Ms. Ly asks her students to respond to the following RAFT:

R   person attending the Gettysburg dedication
A   family member
F   personal letter
T   Lincoln's message

Projects and Performances

On a larger scale, teachers can use projects and performances to check for understanding. Importantly, it is not done at the end when the project has been completed but rather as students work on these types of activities. There is a wide range of appropriate projects and performances that allow students an opportunity to engage in meaningful work aligned with content standards. As one example, Ms. Anderson's English class was focused on the essential question, "What's worth fighting, or even dying, for?" The students in this class wrote an essay in response to the question, read books such as *Romeo and Juliet*, and engaged in class debates. As one project, students created Facebook pages devoted to a worthy cause they

Video 6.3

Sample student debate.
resources.corwin.com/ rigorousreadingtx

would be willing to fight for. As they worked, Ms. Anderson viewed their pages in progress and met with individual students to check their understanding about the essential question. Micah created a page about CHARGE Syndrome, a rare genetic condition that his sister has. As he met with Ms. Anderson, Micah said, "I would fight for money to figure out what causes CHARGE and how to prevent it, I really would." Their discussion provided Ms. Anderson with evidence of Micah's developing understanding of worthy causes. Interestingly, Micah received a message on his Facebook cause page from a parent whose child with CHARGE Syndrome had died 17 years previously thanking him for his efforts.

Tests

Although tests are typically considered a summative assessment tool used for grading, they can also be used to check for understanding. Incorrect answers on a test provide teachers with information about what students still need to learn. Tests can be developed in a number of different formats, ranging from multiple choice to dichotomous choice (true/false, yes/no, agree/disagree) to essays. For example, on the following true/false question, 60% of the students answered incorrectly, informing their teacher that they are confused about some aspect of the life cycle of stars:

> As a star ages, its internal composition changes as nuclear
> reactions in the star's core convert one element into another.

Once the data are collected, teachers have to make decisions. The remainder of this chapter focuses on providing students feedback and making future instructional decisions based on the information

Providing Effective Feedback

Most of us have experienced poor feedback during our learning lives. The teacher who scrawled "rewrite this" in the margin of an essay we had written. The coach who told us, "No, you're doing it wrong, keep practicing." The coworker who took over the project and finished it for us when our progress stalled. The frustration on the learner's part matches that felt by the teacher, coach, or coworker: Why can't he or she get this? That mutual vexation produces a mutual sense of defeat. On the part of the learner, the internal dialogue becomes, "I can't do this." For the teacher, it's, "I can't teach this." Over time, blame sets in, and the student and teacher begin to find fault with each other.

Hattie and Timperley (2007) wrote about feedback across four dimensions: "Feedback about the task (FT), about the processing of the task (FP), about self-regulation (FR), and about the self as a person (FS)" (p. 90).

For example, *"You need to put a semicolon in this sentence"* (FT) has limited usefulness and is not usually generalized to other tasks.

On the other hand, *"Make sure that your sentences have noun-verb agreements because it's going make it easier for the reader to understand your argument"* (FP) gives feedback information about a writing convention necessary in all essays.

The researchers go on to note that feedback that moves from information about the process to information about self-regulation is the best of all. Such feedback might include something like the following: *"Try reading some of your sentences aloud so you can hear when you have and don't have noun-verb agreement."*

The researchers go on to say that FS is the least useful (*"You're a good student"*) even when it is positive in nature because it doesn't add anything to one's learning. A summary of the types of feedback can be found in Figure 6.1.

Done carefully, FT can have a modest amount of usefulness, as when editing a paper. Yet feedback about the task is by far the most common kind we offer. The problem is that the task-related feedback offers only endgame analysis and leaves the learner with little direction on what to do, particularly when there isn't any recourse to make changes. Most writing teachers will tell you that it is not uncommon for students to engage in limited revision, confined to the specific items listed in the teacher feedback—which then makes it more of an exercise in recopying than in revising. However, feedback about the processes used in the task, and further advice about the self-regulatory strategies one can use to make revisions, can leave the learner with a plan for next steps.

Consider the dialogue between English teacher Mark Harris and Alicia, a student in his class. Alicia has drafted an essay on bullying, and John is providing feedback about her work. Careful to frame his feedback so that it can result in a plan for revision, he draws her attention to her thesis statement and says, "It's helpful for writers to go back to the main point of the essay and read to see if the evidence is there. I highlight in yellow so I can see if I've done that." The two of them reread her first three paragraphs and highlight where she has provided national statistics and direct quotes from teachers she knows. "Now what I want you to do is to

The problem is that the task-related feedback offers only endgame analysis and leaves the learner with little direction on what to do, particularly when there isn't any recourse to make changes.

Figure 6.1 Feedback Examples

Type	Example	Usefulness
Feedback about the task (FT)	"Make sure to change this from a period to an exclamation mark."	Limited
Feedback about the processing of the task (FP)	"You seem to want to emphasize this point. Be sure to use a strong verb to capture that intensity so your reader understands this as well."	Very useful
Feedback about self-regulation (FR)	"Read that passage aloud after you rewrite it to yourself to see if it matches the level of intensity you intend."	Very useful
Feedback about the self as a person (Fs)	"Good boy."	Not useful

look for ways you've provided supporting evidence, like through citing sources. Let's highlight those in green." Alicia quickly notices that while she has made claims, she hasn't capitalized on any authoritative sources. As well, by confining her direct quotes to teachers at her school, she has limited the impact of her essay by failing to quote more widely known sources. The little bit of green on her essay illustrates what she needs to do next: strengthen her sources. "It sounds like you have a plan for revising the content. Let's meet again on Wednesday and you can update me on your progress."

Feedback of this nature takes a few minutes yet can add up quickly in a crowded classroom. For this reason, many teachers rely on written forms of feedback as a substitute for direct conversations. Even when providing feedback in written form, the guidelines described above remain the same: Focus on the processes needed for the task, move to information about behaviors that are within the student's influence to change, and steer clear of comments that are either too global or too minute to be of much use. Wiggins (1998) advises constructing written feedback so that it meets four important criteria. First, it must be timely so that it is paired as closely as possible with the attempt; second, it should be specific in nature; third, it should be written in a manner that it understandable to the student; and fourth, it should be actionable so that the learner can make revisions.

While feedback is primarily offered at the individual level, the concept of feeding-up *refers to the process of making instructional decisions about what should happen next for the class as a whole.*

Engaging in Feed-Forward Instruction

While feedback is primarily offered at the individual level, the concept of *feeding-up* refers to the process of making instructional decisions about what should happen next for the class as a whole (Frey & Fisher, 2011). Data about student progress are commonly gathered using common formative assessments that are either commercially produced or teacher-made. In addition, many school teams engage in consensus scoring with colleagues to calibrate assessment practices, especially those associated with tasks that have a significant qualitative component, such as writing (Fisher, Frey, Farnan, Fearn, & Petersen, 2004). However, consensus scoring requires time for colleagues to work together—something that can be hard to come by and can therefore be a limitation to these practices. The good news is that one's own classroom can also serve as the unit of analysis for formative assessment.

With all of the solid feedback provided to students, it seems natural to take this one step further by recording results and doing some pattern analysis. For example, second-grade teacher Elena Vitsen conferred with students during their independent reading to check on their progress toward meeting the standard that students "discuss the author's use of print and graphic features to achieve specific purposes."

"I've been working with them on how we use images, captions, and subheadings to scan and locate information in texts," she explained. "I've been checking in with them about using their science textbook this way."

Consensus scoring requires time for colleagues to work together—something that can be hard to come by and can therefore be a limitation to these practices.

She selects an unfamiliar passage from the book and asks questions about the content of the caption and image, as well as its relation to the main portion of the text. "I'm especially interested right now in whether they are able to accurately predict the content of the passage and figure out where the image belongs," she said. Her error analysis sheet is in Figure 6.2.

Unlike a checklist to track mastery, this error analysis sheet is used to identify and highlight those who are struggling. She logs the initials of students who are still having difficulty with major concepts despite initial instruction, then makes decisions about follow-up and reteaching. For example, the error analysis sheet showed her that almost the entire class was still having difficulty relating the visual to the correct passage. That tells her that reteaching to the whole group is in order. On the other hand, smaller groups of students were having trouble with other concepts:

> I was surprised that I still had a few who aren't using bold words effectively. We've had lots of experiences with these, and I thought everyone had it. I'll need to pull those students into a small group, because the majority of the class is doing fine otherwise.

She will plan further scaffolded instruction for these small groups.

Seventh-grade English teacher Kari McGee is also concerned with examining her students' progress toward informational reading, specifically the expectation that students "analyze how the use of text structure contributes to the author's purpose." Ms. McGee knows that her students need to understand text structures and how they help readers understand the author's purpose. She also knows that her students' writing will improve when they understand the relationship between structure and purpose. "They're writing longer research papers now, but they haven't been applying much in the way of formal and logical organization to their own work, even though we read articles that use these methods," he said. She decided to require students to include some structural analysis of the texts they were reading. "We started with some more obvious ones, such as opinion pieces with titles that included phrases like 'Pros and Cons,'" he said. "As we did close readings, I made sure to spend time on the structures the writer used, and how he laid out his argument." Her students read several articles about space junk. These articles presented a number of different solutions to the

Video 6.4

Daily checks for understanding help teachers identify instructional needs.
resources.corwin.com/ rigorousreadingtx

Video 6.5

A teacher discusses his use of error analysis.
resources.corwin.com/ rigorousreadingtx

Figure 6.2 Grade 2 Error Analysis of Print and Graphic Features

Task	Initials of Students Who Are Having Difficulty With This Skill
Locates caption	
Reads caption and relates it to the text	
Reads caption and relates it to the visual information	
Locates bold word	
Describes the role of bold words	
Finds meaning of bold word using glossary	
Locates subheading	
Describes content expected in the section based on the subheading	
Identifies appropriate visual/graphic and caption related to the text in a subheading	

Video 6.6

Teacher reteaches students to use evidence after the error analysis revealed a need.
resources.corwin.com/ rigorousreadingtx

problem of debris in space and were written by authors from a number of different countries. Her students analyzed the degree to which each writer organized his or her argument sufficiently such that a reader could logically follow the text. "This has been tough for them to do, because they're so sure that if something's published it must automatically be well written." Mr. Laughlin adds the initials of the students in each period who are still struggling with this, so that he can follow up with them:

> They'll need some more scaffolded reading instruction, but it's not like the whole class does. My problem is that I see 180 kids a day, and it gets hard to remember who needs more teaching. Keeping track lets me see who should be in a needs-based group.

Mr. Laughlin's error analysis sheet is in Figure 6.3.

▶ Summary

We are changed by text. We use complex texts to bring the world into our classrooms. But students' potential for learning remains untapped until we provide them with culminating assessments that are equally as complex as the texts they are reading. The texts you choose should serve as a platform for extending ideas and building curiosity. But how do you know if students understand the texts they are reading, or if they need additional information? Through careful observation. What we hear students say during discussion, or read in their writing, sparks further understanding about what should come next. In this way, student assessment never ends until the very last day of school. Caring teachers apply what they have learned about their students to future instruction. They use feedback in ways that build student understanding, and they look for the patterns that will inform their next instructional moves. It is much in the manner of the sheep tender looking over the flock. According to Brick (1908),

> The man who does not like sheep, and who is not willing to devote lots of time to their care . . . has no business meddling with the Spring Lamb . . . To be successful, he must also be gentle, with a watchful eye for little things . . . and a hundred minor details upon which success depends. (p. 154)

Figure 6.3 Grade 7 Error Analysis of Text Structure and Author's Purpose

Task	Initials of Students Who Did Not Demonstrate This Skill				
	Period 1	Period 2	Period 3	Period 4	Period 5
Names appropriate text structure					
Identifies evidence from the text to support the structure					
Discusses the development of ideas related to the structure					
Notes signal words that are consistent with the structure					
Describes one section of the text and its relationship to the author's purpose					
Describes a second section of the text and its relationship to the author's purpose					

In short, the tender must also heed the warning Brick delivered almost a century ago: "You can't fatten sheep by weighing them." In the same way, it is through nurturing and feeding our students—and not merely through measuring them—that we provide them with a window through which they can see the world and themselves in the words of others.

Coda

We have come to the end of this book with just a few words left before you close the cover. You have read this book because you care deeply about your craft and your students. We applaud you for that. You know that simply assigning students complex texts and then wishing them well is not going to yield breakthrough results. You also know that teaching is more than test scores. Yes, providing students access to complex texts will improve their achievement on the next generation of assessments. But more than that, accessing complex texts invites students into the scholarly world. This may sound like hyperbole, but we really believe that unlocking complex texts is the most important thing a teacher can do for his or her students. And now that you have read this book, you have the keys in your hands. The access points in this book work. They ensure that students have the experiences, instruction, and support necessary to read and understand the wide range of texts they will encounter throughout their lives.

References

Adler, M. J., & Van Doren, C. (1972). *How to read a book.* New York: Touchstone.

Afflerbach, P., Pearson, P. D., & Paris, S. G. (2008). Clarifying differences between reading skills and reading strategies. *The Reading Teacher, 61*(5), 364–373.

Alexander, P. A., & Jetton, T. L. (2000). Learning from text: A multidimensional and developmental perspective. In M. L. Kamil, P. B. Mosenthal, P. D. Pearson, & R. Barr (Eds.), *Handbook of reading research* (Vol. 3, pp. 285–310). Mahwah, NJ: Erlbaum.

Allington, R. L. (2002). You can't learn much from books you can't read. *Educational Leadership, 60*(3), 16–19.

Anderson, L., Brubaker, N., Alleman-Brooks, J., & Duffy, G. (1985). A qualitative study of seatwork in first-grade classrooms. *Elementary School Journal, 86*, 123–140.

Anderson, R. C., Wilson, P. T., & Fielding, L. G. (1988). Growth in reading and how children spend their time outside school. *Reading Research Quarterly, 23*, 285–303.

Avalos, M. A., Plasencia, A., Chavez, C., & Rascón, J. (2007/2008). Modified guided reading: Gateway to English as a second language and literacy learning. *The Reading Teacher, 61*, 318–329.

Banks, J. A., & Banks, C. A. M. (2012). *Multicultural education: Issues and perspectives* (8th ed.). New York: Wiley.

Baum, L. F. (1900/2000). *The wonderful wizard of Oz.* New York: HarperCollins.

Bennett, N., & Cass, A. (1989). The effects of group composition on group interactive processes and pupil understanding. *British Educational Research Journal, 15*(1), 19–32.

Bonsignore, J. (2001). *Stick out your tongue! Fantastic facts, features, and functions of animal and human tongues.* Atlanta, GA: Peachtree.

Brick, H. (1908). Early spring lambs. *The Farm Journal, 32*(4), 153–154.

Bromley, K. D. (1985). Précis writing and outlining to enhance content learning. *The Reading Teacher, 38*(4), 406–411.

Brown, A. L., & Day, J. D. (1983). Macrorules for summarizing texts: The development of expertise. *Journal of Verbal Learning and Verbal Behavior, 22*, 1–14.

Buehl, D. (2009). *Classroom strategies for interactive learning* (3rd ed.). Newark, DE: International Reading Association.

Campbell, J. R., Voelkl, K. E., & Donahue, P. L. (1997). *NAEP 1996 trends in academic progress* (Report No. NCES-97-986). Princeton, NJ: National Assessment of Educational Progress. (ERIC Document Reproduction Service No. ED411327)

Carle, E. (1996). *The grouchy ladybug.* New York: HarperCollins.

Carroll, C. (1997). *How artists see families.* New York: Abbeville Kids.

Cazden, C. B. (2001). *Classroom discourse: The language of teaching and learning.* Portsmouth, NH: Heinemann.

Cisneros, S. (1991). *Woman hollering creek, and other stories.* New York: Random House.

Clay, M. M. (2001). *Change over time in children's literacy development.* Portsmouth, NH: Heinemann.

Clements, A. (1996). *Frindle.* New York: Aladdin.

Daniels, H. (2002). *Literature circles: Voice and choice in book clubs and reading groups* (2nd ed.). York, ME: Stenhouse.

Davey, B. (1983). Think aloud: Modeling the cognitive processes for reading comprehension. *Journal of Reading, 27,* 44–47.

Dean, C. B., Stone, B. J., Hubbell, E., & Pitler, H. (2012). *Classroom instruction that works: Research-based strategies for increasing student achievement* (2nd ed.). Alexandria, VA: ASCD.

Donovan, M. S., & Bransford, J. D. (Eds.). (2005). *How students learn: Science in the classroom.* Washington, DC: National Academies Press.

Duffy, G. G. (2014). *Explaining reading: A resource for teaching concepts, skills, and strategies* (3rd ed.). New York: Guilford.

Elbaum, B., Schumm, J. S., & Vaughn, S. (1997). Urban middle-elementary students' perceptions of grouping formats for reading instruction. *Elementary School Journal, 97,* 475–500.

Elley, W. B. (2000). The potential of book floods for raising literary levels. *International Review of Education, 46*(3–4), 233–255.

Fang, Z. (2012). Approaches to developing content area literacies: A synthesis and critique. *Journal of Adolescent & Adult Literacy, 56*(2), 103–108.

Faust, M. A., & Glenzer, N. (2000). "I could read those parts over and over": Eighth graders rereading to enhance enjoyment and learning with literature. *Journal of Adolescent & Adult Literacy, 44,* 234–239.

Fisher, D., & Frey, N. (2008). *Better learning for structured teaching: A framework for the gradual release of responsibility.* Alexandria, VA: ASCD.

Fisher, D., & Frey, N. (2010a). *Enhancing RTI: How to ensure success with effective classroom instruction and intervention*. Alexandria, VA: ASCD.

Fisher, D., & Frey, N. (2010b). *Guided instruction: How to develop confident and successful learners*. Alexandria, VA: ASCD.

Fisher, D., & Frey, N. (2012a). Close reading in elementary schools. *The Reading Teacher, 66,* 179–188.

Fisher, D., & Frey, N. (2012b). *Improving adolescent literacy: Content area strategies at work* (3rd ed.). Boston: Allyn & Bacon.

Fisher, D., & Frey, N. (2013a). *Better learning through structured teaching: A framework for the gradual release of responsibility* (2nd ed.). Alexandria, VA: ASCD.

Fisher, D., & Frey, N. (2013b). *Common Core English language arts in a PLC at work: Grades 3–5*. Bloomington, IN: Solution Tree.

Fisher, D., & Frey, N. (2014). *Checking for understanding: Formative assessment techniques for your classroom* (2nd ed.). Alexandria, VA: ASCD.

Fisher, D., Flood, J., Lapp, D., & Frey, N. (2004). Interactive read alouds: Is there a common set of implementation practices? *The Reading Teacher, 58,* 8–17.

Fisher, D., Frey, N., & Hattie, J. (2016). *Visible learning for literacy: Implementing the practices that work best to accelerate student learning*. Thousand Oaks, CA: Corwin.

Fisher, D., Frey, N., & Lapp, D. (2008). *In a reading state of mind: Brain research, teacher modeling, and comprehension instruction*. Newark, DE: International Reading Association.

Fisher, D., Frey, N., & Lapp, D. (2016). *Text complexity: Stretching readers with texts and tasks*. Thousand Oaks, CA: Corwin.

Fisher, D., Frey, N., & Rothenberg, C. (2008). *Content area conversations: How to plan discussion-based lessons for diverse language learners*. Alexandria, VA: ASCD.

Fisher, D., Frey, N., Farnan, N., Fearn, L., & Petersen, F. (2004). Increasing writing achievement in an urban middle school. *Middle School Journal, 36*(2), 21–26.

Fisher, D., Lapp, D., & Frey, N. (2011). Comprehension: The cooperation of many forces. In D. Lapp & D. Fisher (Eds.), *Handbook of research on teaching the English language arts* (3rd ed.) (pp. 258–263). New York: Routledge.

Fisher, D., Ross, D., & Grant, M. (2010). Building background knowledge in physical science. *The Science Teacher, 77*(1), 23–26.

Fleischman, P. (2006). *Dateline: Troy*. Somerville, MA: Candlewick.

Fountas, I., & Pinnell, G. (2012). Guided reading: The romance and the reality. *The Reading Teacher, 66*(4), 268–284.

Frey, N., & Fisher, D. (2010). Identifying instructional moves during guided learning. *The Reading Teacher, 64*(2), 84–95.

Frey, N., & Fisher, D. (2011). *The formative assessment action plan: Practical steps to more successful teaching and learning.* Alexandria, VA: ASCD.

Frey, N., Fisher, D., & Everlove, S. (2009). *Productive group work: How to engage students, build teamwork, and promote understanding.* Alexandria, VA: ASCD.

Gibson, F. (1956). *Old yeller.* New York: HarperCollins.

Good, T. L., & Brophy, J. E. (2003). *Looking in classrooms* (9th ed.). Boston: Allyn & Bacon.

Graff, G., & Birkenstein, C. (2006). *They say / I say: The moves that matter in academic writing.* New York: W. W. Norton & Company.

Gregory, K. (2001). *Seeds of hope: The gold rush diary of Susanna Fairchild (Dear America).* New York: Scholastic.

Guthrie, J. T., & Wigfield, A. (2000). Engagement and motivation in reading. In M. L. Kamil, P. B. Mosenthal, P. D. Pearson, & R. Barr (Eds.), *Handbook of reading research* (Vol. 3, pp. 403–424). Mahwah, NJ: Erlbaum.

Guthrie, J. T., Hoa, A.L.W., Wigfield, A., Tonks, S. M., Humenick, N. M., & Littles, E. (2007). Reading motivation and reading comprehension growth in the later elementary years. *Contemporary Educational Psychology, 32*(3) 282–313.

Guthrie, J. T., Schafer, W. D., & Huang, C. (2001). Benefits of opportunity to read and balanced instruction on the NAEP. *Journal of Educational Research, 94,* 145–162.

Harvey, V. S., & Chickie-Wolf, L. A. (2007). *Fostering independent learning: Practical strategies to promote student success.* New York: Guilford.

Hattie, J., & Timperley, H. (2007). The power of feedback. *Review of Educational Research, 77,* 81–112.

Hattie, J.A.C., & Donoghue, G. M. (2016). Learning strategies: A synthesis and conceptual model. *Science of Learning, 1.* doi:10.1038/npjscilearn2016.

Hesse, K. (1996). *The music of dolphins.* New York: Scholastic.

Hiebert, E. H. (Ed.). (2009). *Reading more, reading better: Solving problems in the teaching of literacy.* New York: Guilford.

Hill, J. D., & Flynn, K. M. (2006). *Classroom instruction that works with English language learners.* Alexandria, VA: Association for Supervision and Curriculum Development.

Holdaway, D. (1979). *The foundations of literacy.* Portsmouth, NH: Heinemann.

Hua, W., Cromwell, A. M., & McClarty, K. L. (2016). Career readiness: An analysis of text complexity for occupational reading materials. *Journal of Educational Research, 109*(3), 266–274.

Hudson, A. (2016). Get them talking! Using student-led book talks in the primary grades. *The Reading Teacher, 70*(2), 221–225.

Hunter, M. C. (1976). *Improved instruction.* Thousand Oaks, CA: Corwin.

Iowa State University. (2007, May 31). Psychologist explains teens' risky decision-making behavior. *ScienceDaily.* Retrieved from http://www.sciencedaily.com / releases/2007/05/070531093830.htm

Johnson, D. W., Johnson, R. T., & Holubec, E. J. (2008). *Cooperation in the classroom* (8th ed.). Edina, MN: Interaction.

Johnson, D., Johnson, R., Holubec, E. J., & Roy, P. (1984). *Circles of learning: Cooperation in the classroom.* Alexandria, VA: ASCD.

Kafka, F. (1946). *Metamorphosis.* New York: Vanguard Press.

Kapur, M. (2008). Productive failure. *Cognition and Instruction, 26*(3), 379–424.

Klinger, J. K., & Vaughn, S. (1998). Using collaborative strategic reading. *TEACHING Exceptional Children, 30*(6), 32–37.

Klinger, J. K., Vaughn, S., & Schumm, J. S. (1998). Collaborative strategic reading during social studies in heterogeneous fourth-grade classrooms. *Elementary School Journal, 99,* 3–20.

Kush, J. C., & Watkins, M. W. (1996). Long-term stability of children's attitudes toward reading. *Journal of Educational Research, 89,* 315–319.

Lobel, A. (1971). *Frog and toad together.* New York: HarperCollins.

Lord, W. (1955). *A night to remember.* New York: St. Martin's Griffin.

Lowry, L. (1989). *Number the stars.* New York: Laurel Leaf.

Manzo, A. (1969). ReQuest: A method for improving reading comprehension through reciprocal questioning. *Journal of Reading, 12,* 123–126.

Marinak, B. A., & Gambrell, L. B. (2016). *No more reading for junk: Best practices for motivating readers.* Portsmouth, NH: Heinemann.

Marzano, R. J. (2009). *Designing & teaching learning goals and objectives.* Bloomington, IN: Solution Tree.

Marzano, R. J., Pickering, D. J., & Pollock, J. E. (2002). *Classroom instruction that works: Research-based strategies for increasing student achievement.* Alexandria, VA: Association for Supervision and Curriculum Development.

Matthews, M. W., & Kesner, J. (2003). Children learning with peers: The confluence of peer status and literacy competence within small-group literacy events. *Reading Research Quarterly, 38*, 208–234.

McLaughlin, M., & DeVoogd, G. L. (2004). *Critical literacy: Enhancing students' comprehension of text*. New York: Scholastic.

Millis, K. K., & King, A. (2001). Rereading strategically: The influences of comprehension ability and a prior reading on the memory for expository text. *Reading Psychology, 22*, 41–65.

Neuman, S. (2017). The information book flood: Is additional exposure enough to support early literacy development? *The Elementary School Journal, 118*(1), 1–27.

Newkirk, T. (2010). The case for slow reading. *Educational Leadership, 67*(6), 6–11.

Optiz, M. F., & Rasinski, T. V. (2008). *Good-bye round robin: 25 effective oral reading strategies* (updated ed.). Portsmouth, NH: Heinemann.

Palincsar, A. S., & Brown, A. L. (1984). Reciprocal teaching of comprehension-fostering and comprehension-monitoring activities. *Cognition and Instruction, 1*(2), 117–175.

Pearson, P. D., & Fielding, L. (1991). Comprehension instruction. In R. Barr, M. L. Kamil, P. Mosenthal, & P. D. Pearson (Eds.), *Handbook of reading research* (Vol. 2, pp. 815–860). Mahwah, NJ: Erlbaum.

Pearson, P. D., & Gallagher, M. C. (1983). The instruction of reading comprehension. *Contemporary Educational Psychology, 8*, 317–344.

Pinkney, J. (2009). *The lion and the mouse*. New York: Little, Brown.

Pinnell, G. S., & Fountas, I. C. (2003). Teaching comprehension. *The California Reader, 36*(4), 7–14.

Pressley, M., El-Dinary, P. B., Gaskins, I., Schuder, T., Bergman, J. L., Almasi, J., et al. (1992). Beyond direct explanation: transactional instruction of reading comprehension strategies. *The Elementary School Journal, 92*, 513–555.

Richards, I. A. (1929). *Practical criticism*. London: Cambridge University Press.

Rog, L. J. (2001). *Early literacy instruction in kindergarten*. Newark, DE: International Reading Association.

Rosenblatt, L. M. (1938/1995). *Literature as exploration* (5th ed.). New York: Modern Language Association.

Rosenblatt, L. M. (2003). Literary theory. In J. Flood, D. Lapp, J. R. Squire, & J. M. Jensen (Eds.), *Handbook of research on teaching the English language arts* (pp. 67–73). New York: Macmillan.

Ryan, P. M. (1999). *Riding freedom*. New York: Scholastic.

Santa, C. M, & Havens, L. T. (1995). *Project CRISS: Creating independence through student-owned strategies*. Dubuque, IA: Kendall/Hunt.

Santa, C., & Havens, L. (1995). *Creating independence through student-owned strategies: Project CRISS*. Dubuque, IA: Kendall Hunt.

Schunk, D. H. (1998). Goal and self-evaluative influences during children's cognitive skill learning. *American Educational Research Journal, 33,* 359–382.

Schunk, D. H., Meece, J. R., & Pintrich, P. R. (2013). *Motivation in education: Theory, research, and applications* (4th ed.). Boston, MA: Pearson.

Sendak, M. (1963). *Where the wild things are.* New York: Harper & Rowe.

Smith, M. C. (1950, June 1). *Declaration of conscience.* US Congress, Senate, Congressional Record, 81st Congress, 2d sess., 7894–7895. Retrieved from http:// www. americanrhetoric.com/speeches/margaretchasesmithconscience.html

Smith, M. C. (2000). The real-world reading practices of adults. *Journal of Literacy Research, 32,* 25–52.

Spinelli, J. (2003). *Stargirl.* New York: Scholastic.

Stanovich, K. E. (1986). Matthew effects in reading: Some consequences of individual differences in the acquisition of literacy. *Reading Research Quarterly, 21,* 360–407.

Steinbeck, J. (1945). *The pearl.* New York: Penguin Books.

Stright, A. D., & Supplee, L. H. (2002). Children's self-regulatory behaviors during teacher-directed, seat-work, and small-group instructional contexts, *Journal of Educational Research, 95,* 235–246.

Tatham, B. (2002). *How animals shed their skin.* New York: Franklin Watts.

Tayback, S. (1999). *Joseph had a little overcoat.* New York: Viking.

Tayback, S. (2007). *There was an old lady who swallowed a fly.* Auburn, ME: Child's Play International.

Trivizas, E. (1993). *The three little wolves and the big bad pig.* New York: Aladdin.

Vygotsky, L. S. (1978). *Mind in society: The development of higher psychological processes* (M. Cole, V. John-Steiner, S. Scribner, & E. Souberman, Eds. & Trans.). Cambridge, MA: Harvard University Press.

Weber, K. (Ed.). (2012). *Last call at the oasis: The global water crisis and where we go from here.* New York: PublicAffairs.

Wiesel, E. (1982). *Night.* New York: Bantam.

Wiggins, G. (1998). *Educative assessment: Designing assessments to inform and improve student performance.* San Francisco: Jossey-Bass.

Wiggins, G., & McTighe, J. (2005). *Understanding by design* (2nd ed.). Alexandria, VA: ASCD.

Wilhelm, J. D. (2001). Think-alouds boost reading comprehension. *Instructor, 111*(4), 26–28.

Winter, J. (2002). *Frida.* New York: Arthur A. Levine.

Wood, A. (2009). *The napping house*. San Diego: Harcourt Brace.

Wood, D., & Wood, H. (1996). Vygotsky, tutoring and learning. *Oxford Review of Education, 22*(1), 5–16.

Wood, D., Bruner, J. S., & Ross, G. (1976). The role of tutoring in problem solving. *Journal of Child Psychology and Psychiatry, 17*(2), 89–100.

Wozniak, C. L. (2011). Reading and talking about books: A critical foundation for intervention. *Voices From The Middle, 19*(2), 17–21.

Yeager, D., & Dweck, C. (2012). Mindsets that promote resilience: When students believe that personal characteristics can be developed. *Educational Psychologist, 47*(4), 302–314.

Index

CORWIN LITERACY | BECAUSE ALL TEACHERS ARE LEADERS

Do you have a minute? Of course not. That's why at Corwin Literacy we have put together a collection of just-in-time, classroom-tested, practical resources from trusted experts that allow you to quickly find the information you need when you need it.

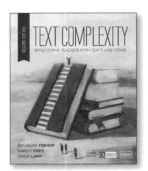

Douglas Fisher, Nancy Frey, Diane Lapp

No matter what discipline you teach, learn how to use complexity as a dynamic, powerful tool for using the right text at just the right time.

Douglas Fisher, Nancy Frey, Russell J. Quaglia, Dominique Smith, Lisa L. Lande

Learn how focusing on relationships, clarity, and challenge can put you in control of managing your classroom's success, one motivated student at a time.

Douglas Fisher, Nancy Frey, Heather Anderson, Marisol Thayre

Learn the best ways to use text-dependent questions as scaffolds during close reading and the big understandings they yield. Includes illustrative video, texts and questions, cross-curricular examples, and online facilitator's guides.

Douglas Fisher, Nancy Frey, Heather Anderson, Marisol Thayre

The questions guide students' engagement and discussion as they consider explicit and implied meanings and analyze and appreciate various aspects of a text.

To

**Douglas Fisher,
Nancy Frey, John Hattie**

Ensure students demonstrate more than a year's worth of learning during a school year by implementing the right literacy practice at the right moment.

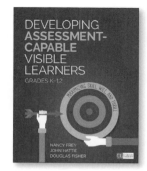

**Nancy Frey,
John Hattie,
Douglas Fisher**

Imagine students who understand their educational goals and monitor their progress. This illuminating book focuses on self-assessment as a springboard for markedly higher levels of student achievement.

**Douglas Fisher,
Nancy Frey,
John Hattie,
Marisol Thayre**

High-impact strategies to use for all you teach—all in one place. Deliver sustained, comprehensive literacy experiences each day.

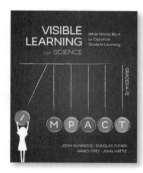

**John Almarode,
Douglas Fisher,
Nancy Frey, John Hattie**

Learn the precise instructional approach to use at each phase of the learning cycle—surface, deep, and transfer—for maximum-impact science teaching.

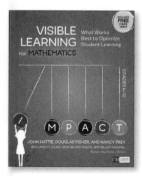

**John Hattie,
Douglas Fisher,
Nancy Frey,
Linda M. Gojak,
Sara Delano Moore,
William Mellman**

By incorporating John Hattie's ground-breaking analysis and common mathematics research, you will have the tools to design powerful, precision learning.

**Nancy Frey,
Douglas Fisher,
Molly Katherine Ness,
Kristine Michele Allen**

By strengthening foundational metacognitive skills, these learner's notebooks guide students to understand what they're learning, why they're learning it, and the strategies they need along the way. These notebooks are available for learners in Grades K–2, 3–5, 6–8, and 9–12. Teacher's guide included with packs of 20.

A SAGE Publishing Company

Helping educators make the greatest impact

CORWIN HAS ONE MISSION: to enhance education through intentional professional learning.

We build long-term relationships with our authors, educators, clients, and associations who partner with us to develop and continuously improve the best evidence-based practices that establish and support lifelong learning.